Under the Workers' Caps

Under the
Workers' Caps

From Champion Mill
to Blue Ridge Paper

GEORGE LOVELAND

The University of Tennessee Press / *Knoxville*

Copyright © 2005 by The University of Tennessee Press /
Knoxville.

All Rights Reserved. Manufactured in the United States
of America.

First Edition.

This book is printed on acid-free paper.

Loveland, George, 1956–
  Under the workers' caps : from Champion Mill to Blue
Ridge Paper / George Loveland.— 1st ed.
    p. cm.
Includes bibliographical references and index.

ISBN 1–57233–365–0 (hardcover)

  1. Employee ownership—United States.
  2. Paper industry workers—United States.
  3. Blue Ridge Paper Products.
  I. Title.

HD5658.P332U67 2005

338.7'676'0973—dc22   2004016496

For Eeth and Caroline

Contents

Illustrations

Preface

In 1997 Champion International Paper Inc. attempted to increase profits by selling off its "nonstrategic assets," all of its holdings that were no longer essential to its primary business. It was the "just-in-time" industrial model of the 1990s, which stressed cutting back overhead in favor of production on demand. The strategy marked a dramatic shift for the Champion empire, which had once been an extensive network of wooded lands that produced chips, processing plants that mulched the chips into pulp, machines that flattened the pulp into paper, and packaging plants that molded the paper into boxes and cartons.

Two of these nonstrategic assets were the paper mills in Canton and Waynesville, North Carolina, known as the Canton system, which Champion put up for sale in October of 1997. It was becoming a familiar story in rural America. Entire towns, whose economic life was hitched to a single industry, suddenly found themselves dying as the blood of their economic life flowed south to Mexico or to other developing nations that offered low-wage workers and little regulation. In the typical story, the town withers and dries up as the young people move away in search of work.

This time, however, something amazing happened. With the employees and families of the Canton system still reeling from the shock of learning that the mills they had operated for four generations were up for sale, a man named Frank Adams showed up on the scene. Adams, founder and president of the Southern Appalachian Center for Cooperative Ownership, Inc. laid out a new possibility. Why not organize through the union to purchase and operate the mills as worker-owners? Later, when he attempted, unsuccessfully, to help an employee buyout in Natchez, Mississippi, Adams was asked what his role was. He replied:

> My job is to organize at least a small group of employee-selected leaders, or as large a group of employees as possible in a particular situation. The challenge is to organize around their hopes, skills, and aspirations, rather than their fears and anger. By organizing this way, no matter the outcome, a group of women and

men, no matter how small or large, gain in their sense of self-worth, and in the belief that they can take on challenges. Even in a failure, as in this case, they say, routinely, that their lives will change for the better.

In the process of becoming worker-owners, employees of the Canton system could grow as individuals and create a democratic workplace culture. It was a lofty vision that went far beyond the goal of maximizing profits for the smallest capital outlay possible. It would require workers to face adversity, meet challenges, learn, grow, and do whatever it would take to see the process through to its conclusion.

Fortunately for the people of Haywood County, North Carolina, and for all of us who are buffeted about by the fickle winds of an indifferent economic system, these "nonstrategic assets" took up the challenge and gave us a new model.

Acknowledgments

In the spring of 1999, Frank Adams, a consultant in one of the largest employee buyouts in history, suggested that I write a book about the experience. Knowing that he had published four, I asked, very tentatively, what writing a book was like. He didn't hesitate. "It's the loneliest work you'll ever do." I can't count the number of times I have reflected on the truth of this comment over the past four years. But the experience has also deepened friendships and professional relationships, which I would like to acknowledge.

I agreed to take up Frank's suggestion if he would give me a place to stay when I was working in Asheville, read the manuscript and give me straightforward critique, and keep my cup full of red wine. In addition to all of this, Frank has been a warm friend, mentor, and teacher. I really can't say if I have learned more from him as a writer or as a teacher, since I soon came to realize that he was helping me in the same ways that he had once helped civil rights workers to organize effectively, Appalachian community activists to find their political voices, and working people to gain the knowledge and skills to buy and operate their own companies. I once commented to Frank that he seemed to take a rather optimistic view of human nature, and he responded firmly, "By God, if you consider yourself an educator you'd BETTER have an optimistic view of human nature!" I have been blessed with the opportunity to be Frank's student. I also treasure his friendship.

Even so, the numerous late-night arrivals in Asheville, days spent in interviews, and mad dashes back to my job in Virginia would have been tedious without the presence of Margaret Adams. Her warm and loving support, wonderful sense of humor, colorfully spun stories, and attentive presence transformed these visits into social events. Thank you, Margaret, for all of the comforts you have so generously shared with me.

Doug Gibson, Daniel Gregg, Richard Haney, Vanise Henson, Alton Higgins, and Kenny Sutton, the six men who are responsible for the story that follows, have affirmed my faith in the potential for true democracy. Since college, when I first embraced the concept that working people are more qualified than bosses or owners to manage the day-to-day production process in factories, mills, offices, and educational institutions, I have been embroiled in arguments and debates. People ask me how workers could possibly know enough about the overall process to make intelligent decisions, how a common laborer with no college could possibly know more than someone with a master's in business administration, or why a worker would even want to get involved in high-level decisions. I have clung to the theory that workers who actually produce the product or service have the most intimate knowledge of the process and so possess a vast untapped store of experiential knowledge. I am thankful to the six men of the Smoky Mountain Local 507 ESOP Committee for affirming the truth of this theory in actual practice. Listening to their stories, filled with wisdom, integrity, and creativity, has been a joy. But functioning as worker-owners takes time and energy, and I am also deeply grateful for the many hours that Doug, Daniel, Richard, Vanise, Alton, and Kenny took away from their jobs to share their stories. I pray that I have woven them into an accurate narrative.

I am grateful to L. J. Rose, PACE International's regional representative in Haywood County at the time that these events took place. L. J. loaned me his journal, a day-by-day documentation of his activities and his dealings with the ESOP Committee, containing carefully recorded detail of meetings, decisions, conversations, and some personal evaluation. This book would be nowhere near as complete or accurate without this remarkable document.

I have been very fortunate to work under Dr. C. I. Dillon, Ferrum College's library director, for the past eight years. Cy has been more of a colleague than a boss, and I thank him for this as well as for embracing my broad vision of what constitutes appropriate research for a college librarian. He has supported my historical and sociological research and has graciously granted me leave time to pursue it. He has also been understanding and helpful as I juggled reference duties with writing and editing. I could never have completed this book without this support.

Cheryl Hundley, Ferrum College's interlibrary loan librarian, has transformed our small college library into a major research university, and I thank her for performing her magic. Other colleagues have provided the professional and emotional support that has made the journey a little less lonely. I would like to recognize a few, in alphabetical order: Kaye Adams, Peggie Barker, Gary Evans, Steve Fisher, Katherine Grimes, Tina Hanlon, Susan Mead, Milt Rowan, John Spataro, Frédéric Torimiro, Lana Whited, and Dan Woods.

It was my mother, Mildred P. Loveland, who first awakened and then nourished my love of language. Perhaps more important for this project, she was also the one who first taught me that there is a difference between fair and unfair and that standing up for fairness is always worth the effort. Without your influence, Mom, I would have had neither the motivation nor the technical skills to tell this story. I love you.

This book is dedicated to my children, Beth and Caroline. You are the reason that this story is so important. In a few short years you will begin a life of work in an economy that may reward your hard work with success and security, but may as likely threaten to destroy your dreams and visions. Here is a model for those hard times. When the powerful and wealthy who control our society threaten to take all you have, remember that you share with others a power to create a new more just, and equitable order.

CHAPTER 1

Nonstrategic Assets

On October 7, 1997, Vanise Henson and other leaders of United Paperworkers International Union, Local 507, waited for a conference call with Richard Olson, their company's chief executive officer. Champion International Paper, which had operated in Canton, North Carolina, since 1908, was expected to announce a major restructuring plan.

Henson, a vice-president at the local, with thirty-nine years in the nearby Waynesville plant, was only slightly concerned. He thought the restructuring might involve a few job combinations, some departmental transfers, maybe even some jobs lost to attrition. He regretted this. It would mean that his children and grandchildren would have less of a chance to land a union job with solid benefits. But at least they would still have some chance. Most jobs would remain, and the secure life that he, his father, and his grandfather had enjoyed would still be an option.

Henson, however, was not naive. He was a paper mill worker in a small southern community, and this was the age of NAFTA. Manufacturing industries were fleeing communities such as his in pursuit of lower wages and less regulation. While he believed that he and his fellow workers were responsible for Champion's tremendous success, Henson accepted the company's claims that it had to make changes to stay competitive.[1]

Alton Higgins, recording secretary of Local 507, was at the union hall that day. Higgins had worked in nearly every part of the paper mill and had been active in the union for most of his working life. For more than twenty years he had studied and analyzed the hundreds of systems and subsystems that operate in a modern paper mill. He had also studied and analyzed the interactions between the humans who operated these technical systems. He was curious about Champion's announcement, speculating to himself about how the restructuring might affect production. Like Henson, he was slightly uneasy about how the changes might impact the community. But he was also eager to tackle the challenges of making new systems work efficiently.[2]

Daniel Gregg's great-grandfather had logged timber at nearby Lake Logan, helping to produce the very first dollar of profit that Champion cleared in Canton. Gregg, a vice-president at Local 507, was not with Henson and Higgins on the conference call, but he had heard the talk of the proposed restructuring. When he opened his *Asheville Citizen-Times* the following morning, he was hoping finally to learn just what the plans were.[3] Doug Gibson, with more than twenty-five years seniority at Champion, was keeping a watchful eye on the television news.[4] Richard Haney, a key organizer in the successful 1966 campaign that won union recognition for Champion's workers, stopped by the union hall, where someone handed him a printout of an Internet news story.[5]

Business Wire, an online news service, told the story in such sterile terms that Haney had to read between the lines to figure out exactly what had happened. Shareholders were comforted with the news that "Champion International Corporation today announced a three-pronged strategy to maximize total shareholder return by focusing on strategic businesses, increasing profitability, and improving financial discipline." Gregg's *Citizen-Times* left no doubt about what it meant to be designated a "non-strategic facility." The one-inch-tall, bold headline read "Canton Mill for Sale."[6]

Henson was stunned when the CEO explained that the two western North Carolina mills were being put up for sale. He later recalled feelings of fear and uncertainty. "Here I've got thirty-nine years' service. I didn't know what was going to happen. Who was going to buy it? Would they run it? Would they shut it down?"[7]

Higgins remembered everyone in the union hall "sitting there in shock" at Champion's announcement. "We were saying to ourselves, 'what's going to happen to us?' and 'what does this mean to us?' and 'what's the future hold for us?'" The confusion and shock lasted for "three or four days," and was "a very high emotional period." Higgins felt his community and the security of a good job being ripped away from him. "Does this mean I've got to move out of western North Carolina?" he wondered. "Is there a job out there for me? Will a big paper company come in and buy us? And if they do come in and buy us does that mean . . . there will be a huge decrease in wages? How will this impact my life?"[8]

Gregg felt betrayed. For more than ninety years, since before the Canton mill was even completed, his family had created profits for Champion. He remembered that the news "didn't settle too well. It was a very stressful time for everybody." Two years later, Gregg could not conceal a trace of bitterness in his voice when he recalled that Champion had characterized the Canton and Waynesville mills as "non-strategic assets." "It did hurt quite a bit," he said.[9]

Haney also felt betrayed. "Over the years, I knew we were making money." The company had consistently upped its production demands, and Haney took pride in the fact that Canton and Waynesville had just as consistently met the challenge. "Seems like every time we heard anything, it was 'we need more and more and more.'" So in spite of the fact that he had seen "some indications three or four days prior" to the announcement, "it still came as a surprise . . . a shock."[10]

When Doug Gibson heard the story on the television news, he tried to analyze the situation carefully and philosophically. "I thought, well, they're going to sell us off. Now who are they going to try to sell us to? Who would be out there in the world marketplace who would want something like this?" The answer did not comfort him. "And if you look at it and really think about it a lot, nobody would want it." He feared that one of Champion's competitors would purchase the mills intending to shut them down. "If you have a big share of the market already, and you can reduce some of the competition, shut the facilities over here at Canton down, you're doing two things. You're shutting your competition down and you're better positioning yourself in the market."[11]

Kenny Sutton was tired of life as a paper mill worker, and had been looking for a way out. "I was disenchanted with it. I was just absolutely wore out with it," he said. "I wanted to be that guy that goes in and does his job and gets the hell out." Still, he described the same shock that the others had felt when, "totally out of left field, Champion came up and said Canton is not strategic. It took the mill manager by surprise, it took the management by surprise, and it took all of us by surprise."

In spite of his desire to go in a new direction, he was terrified when he thought about losing the security of his job at Champion: "I remember lying in bed that night scared to death, thinking, 'what the hell am I gonna do? I'm forty-five years old, what am I gonna do now?' Absolutely, literally scared to death. Like I know a lot of people were. They may admit it; they may not, but I know a lot of people were scared. 'What's gonna happen to me? This is all I've done since I've been in my twenties, so what the hell am I gonna do?'"[12]

When Henson, Higgins, Haney, Gregg, Gibson, and Sutton describe their feelings at learning that Champion intended to sell its Canton and Waynesville paper mills, they use the language of grief over news that struck them and their fellow workers like a sudden and unexpected death. They reacted first with denial. "It can't be. It is just a marketing strategy. They would never do this to us." When they could no longer deny the numerous deaths they were facing, deaths of their family traditions, their community's cohesiveness, their economically and socially secure lives, their dreams for their children, denial gave way to anger and resentment. Some moved on to the bargaining stage, where they told themselves that if only Champion would give them one more chance they could prove that they could be profitable. Some gave in to depression, where they felt overwhelmed with the hard reality that they stood to lose everything. This story is of six men who moved beyond the denial, the fears, and the depression into a liberating acceptance of the situation that enabled them to transform a potential disaster into a new opportunity for themselves, their families, and their entire community. It is the story of how these men transformed themselves into strategic assets.

CHAPTER 2

Smoky Mountain Local 507

North Carolina is a right-to-work state where, in 1996, the year before the Canton and Waynesville mills went up for sale, only 4.1 percent of the workforce was organized.[1] Given the state's antiunion climate, it is somewhat surprising that Smoky Mountain Local 507 exists at all. The local was chartered in 1966, but its roots reach all the way back to local labor struggles of the late nineteenth century.

The Western North Carolina Central Labor Council was founded in 1881, the same year that the groundwork was laid for a national labor federation.[2] After a national conference held in Terre Haute, Indiana, failed to unify locals scattered throughout the country, a second was held later the same year in Pittsburgh. It appealed to working-class consciousness and solidarity as a force to check the growing power of big business. "Fellow-workingmen," the announcement began, "the time has now arrived for a more perfect combination of Labor—one that will concentrate our forces so as to more successfully cope with concentrated capital."[3] This interest in organizing across industries rather than by craft or trade was reflected in the Western North Carolina Central Labor Council, which included some of the nation's first organized electrical workers, painters, barkeeps, retail clerks, and bricklayers.[4]

Unionists in other parts of the country were not as effective at organizing across industries, and this second attempt at national unity produced little more than internal squabbles and bickering. In 1886 a third call went out for a convention to bring "the bonds of unity much closer together between all the trades unions of America."[5] This conference was held in Columbus, Ohio, and delegates from western North Carolina were on hand. By the conference's end they had forged a new organization, the American Federation of Labor (AFL). The North Carolina delegates helped draft and ratify a constitution that proclaimed "a struggle is going on in all the nations of the civilized world, between the capitalist and laborer." The AFL's role in this class struggle would be to nurture "the encouragement and formation of local Trades and Labor Unions and the closer Federation of such societies."[6]

In 1888 many of western North Carolina's unionized workers hired on with George Vanderbilt, a grandson of the shipping magnate Cornelius Vanderbilt, to construct the Biltmore House in Asheville. Vanderbilt, always eager to impress others of his class with a show of opulence, had purchased 125,000 acres and commissioned a mansion with 250 rooms and a seventy-four-feet by forty-two-feet banquet hall.[7] The six-year project employed more than one thousand workers, many of them electricians, painters, and bricklayers represented by the same unions who were present at the AFL's founding convention.[8]

WNC Central Labor Council records indicate that by 1896 the area's unionized workforce included stonemasons, plumbers, plasterers, painters, electrical workers, carpenters, joiners, and bricklayers.[9] So in 1906, when the founder and president of Champion Fibre Company, Peter Thompson, chose Haywood County, North Carolina, as an ideal location for a pulp and paper operation, he inherited a workforce that was familiar with the principles of unionism and working-class struggle.

Thompson hired a young lawyer named Reuben B. Robertson to handle the legal work for the mill in Haywood County. Before long, Robertson married Thompson's daughter and became the mill's president and chairman of the board. The two men arranged a meeting with Frank Gilbreth, whose "scientific management" theory claimed that if physical motion were broken down into intricate detail and unnecessary movements were eliminated, productivity would increase. Thompson was so impressed with Gilbreth's ideas that he offered him a contract to oversee the construction of the Canton mill. In preparing his memoirs, Robertson wrote: "[Gilbreth] claimed great things for the brick laying methods he had developed. . . . There was massive brick work to be done especially on the digester houses where the walls at the foundation level, were three to four feet thick. A more efficient method of laying bricks with better delivery of brick and mortar to the brick layer was accordingly of very great importance from a cost standpoint." In Gilbreth's theory, workers were closer to robots than humans, with movements that could be manipulated and minds that could be programmed to perform repetitive tasks. This approach hit a snag with the Haywood County workers. "The experience under this arrangement was very costly for Champion," Robertson recalled. "Later on the scientific management contractors yielded to 'realities.' . . . The scientific Gilbreth method looked mighty promising while it was being discussed on the lawn at Laurel Court (Gilbreth was a great promoter) but when it came to training the North Carolina brick layers and laborers in these methods it was a wholly different story. In the 'hassle' the local labor won out over the scientists."[10]

Robertson does not comment on the nature of the "hassle" and blames it on "the workers of the region," characterizing them as "mountain farmers who (except for having worked out their road tax on the highways) had never had experience on 'public works' where they were under orders from a 'boss.'"[11] But the workers who had helped charter the AFL and who met regularly through the Western North Carolina Central Labor Council were well acquainted with taking orders from bosses. They also knew that the arbitrary power of a "boss" could be checked by the power of organization. Perhaps it was these experiences that made them resist being treated like automatons.

Using their own skills, rather than management theories, the workers had completed construction of Champion's pulp and paper mill in Canton by the end of 1907, and it began production on January 1, 1908. Robertson had learned from his earlier "hassles" with workers over scientific management theory. He began developing a policy that he called "cooperative goodwill," which he hoped would create a more compliant workforce. Many years later, in a speech to the National Association of Manufacturers, he claimed that he had won industrial peace by understanding what the workers really wanted. "They want *a system for saving for old age,* such as the Social Security plan envisages. They want *opportunity to advance and prosper.* Finally they want an *understanding with the boss.* They want 'cooperation, *not* conflict.'" He had seen a latent power among the workers that could erupt if these needs were ignored. "When workers cannot or will not obtain these satisfactions from management," he said, "they are enticed into finding these satisfactions elsewhere: from unions, from promising politicians, even from radical theorists."[12]

FOR·THE·
PROGESSIVE·TICKET
OF·CANTON·NC·
SUNDAY·

APR·30·—12M·

While many of his fellow industrialists dug in their heels and refused to consider worker demands, Robertson chose a different path He sought to diffuse labor militancy with public displays of concern New employees were required to read *The Champion Guide,* which informed them that "we are known at home and elsewhere as 'The Champion Family,' because of the friendly spirit of co-operation and good fellowship. . . . The underlying principle of the management is a 'Square Deal.' In all of our transactions with you we shall be governed by this principle, and in turn shall expect you to deal fairly with us."[13]

Through "cooperative goodwill" Robertson nourished a loyalty that remains firm to this day. Local 507's president James Hutchinson fondly recalled life in the Champion family nearly thirty years after its patriarch's death. Workers "could go to the community stores up here on the corner above Canton. They could buy things on time. They [Champion] took care of their employees." And in the days when not everyone owned a car, the company "drove them back and forth to work."[14]

Robertson himself personified this ideal. His generosity is legendary. Richard Haney remembered him as "a gentleman from the word go. He talked to the people. He'd come to the mill and they related to him."[15] Charles Cable, Local 507's first president, spoke of the Robertson family as "almost God, as far as the people, the workers, were concerned. And they were good to us. There was no animosity, in the sense of management and labor, as far as I can recall, well before I went to work there."[16] He related to workers as individuals and showed concern for their problems. Hutchinson remembered that when Robertson took one of his frequent walks through the plant, people would "walk up and just say, 'my wife's sick and I don't have enough money to take care of her medicine . . . ,' and [Robertson would] just

---

Left: Workers constructing the Canton mill around 1906 take a break from pile driving, which was necessary for building on the swampy land around the Pigeon River. The inscription reads, in part, "For the Progressive Ticket of Canton, North Carolina," suggesting that class consciousness has long played a part in western North Carolina politics. *Courtesy of the Snug Harbor Photo Archives, Canton. Reprinted with permission.*

write them out a check, or open up his billfold and give them money right there. Because this was his company."[17]

Champion workers drew comfort and security from their close ties to each other through the company. "So we were part of this paternal thing," Cable said. "And we loved it. We did all of our trading at the company store. You bought your wood and your coal and your groceries and your clothes, everything. And it came out of daddy's paycheck. I remember one payday in particular, where daddy drew two cents. The rest of it all came out at the company store. Even your drugs, you could go to the company store and get a slip and go out to the drug store and whatever you got it was charged to daddy. The company had an agreement with all the druggists in town that they were going to pay. It was a wonderful time. It was a depression time, too, during 1933 on to 1940."[18]

It is surprising to find a factory worker remembering the Great Depression as a "wonderful time." Such contentment suggests that Robertson had successfully created an ideal, serene company town shielded from threats of "unionism and radical philosophy." In fact, the ties of the Champion family were so strong that Local 507's first president didn't even begrudge Robertson his huge salary. "I know that while we were in those [dangerous working conditions for relatively low pay] the Robertsons were millionaires; I know that," he said. "But they were millionaires that we liked. They were not millionaires way up in New York City somewhere." Cable described how loyalty to Robertson was even reflected in the building itself. "[Robertson] was well over six feet tall. And one way we'd measure pipelines down in the mill was you'd measure six feet, six inches, or whatever it was so Mr. Robertson could walk under it. I'm telling you the truth. We were building a ridge panel there and Bob [a construction crew worker] was a little better than six feet. He'd hold his hand over his head to make sure it was high enough, because Mr. Robertson would be coming through there sometimes."

Of course such pleasant reveries whitewash history. It is fun to remember the pleasant times and often painful and difficult to remember the struggles. In spite of his fond memories of earlier days in Canton, Cable stops short of nostalgia. "Those were the good old days

Fibreville, the company town that housed Champion workers, reflected Reuben Robertson's attempt to foster a contented workforce. Note the playground in the center and the garden plots behind the homes. *Courtesy of the Snug Harbor Photo Archives, Canton. Reprinted with permission.*

that everybody wants to go back to. I don't want to go back to them because, I tell you, I'd rather have what we got now."[19]

Cable scoffed at an account of life at Champion printed in a 1916 special edition of the *Carolina Mountaineer.* The paper, which was attempting to help entice industry and tourism to the area, proclaimed, "Champion Fibre Employees Look Upon the Great Pulp and Extract Mill at Canton as an Ideal Place to Work—Perfect Harmony and Co-operation Between Employer and Employees."[20] In a related article, the editor of Champion's company newsletter claims to have interviewed three workers who give glowing accounts of the wages, the medical care, and the company's constant solicitation of their opinions. One employee describes a company deeply committed to "safety first": "When accidents happen, however slight, the employee is at once put under care of a competent doctor, or a skilled attendant, and is kept under the care of the doctor until pronounced well. This is without cost to the employee as the doctor is at the well equipped 'First Aid Room' for several hours each day for surgical work and medical consultation. . . . When, despite all precautions, a serious accident happens, the sufferer is rushed to an Asheville hospital and no expense is spared. He is given the benefit of all the medical and surgical skill that money can buy, the Company standing all the expense."[21]

In the plant where the pulp was bleached to produce white paper, "most of the fellows who worked over there coughed all the time," said Cable. "You could tie a string to a rat and try to drag him through that place, and when you went out the other end you'd just have a string. The rat's already gone. You didn't worry about rats in that place. But people worked in that." Cable's boss bore little resemblance to the compassionate supervisors of the *Carolina Mountaineer* account:

> We were down there [at the bleaching plant] one time working, and I tell you it was horrible. We had these little gas masks you can put on over your nose and your mouth, but that doesn't amount to anything. My boss man came by and said, "that's good for you to get in there and breathe a little bit of that [chlorine gas]. That will get rid of your cold." I said, "yeah, I won't have a cold. It's going to kill me, and if I die I won't get a cold." If you'd get a big dose of gas you'd go somewhere and vomit and get over it, get you some sweet milk and drink it and get over it. And that night, maybe, you might not sleep good, but you'd be okay in a day or two.[22]

Aside from chronic health problems, the chemicals used in making paper sometimes caused instant death: "We had five young men killed down there [at the mill] after the union came in. They were clearing out a sewer. The plant had shut down. At that time it shut down maybe once a year for general repairs of the plant. So when they shut down they'd always clean out the sewers. One of [the young men] I remember was a college student. They got in there and the hydrogen sulfide gas came in on them and killed every one of them. My uncle was killed with hydrogen sulfide gas up on top of the evaporator. We've had lots of people killed and crippled for life from one thing or the other."[23]

And as to the company's claims that it always put safety first, Cable said: 'Safety was not first. It never was. It was just a slogan. It didn't mean anything. We had a safety supervisor, and they were good people. I loved every one of them, but they had no authority. They couldn't walk up to a machine supervisor and say, 'now you shut that machine down [for safety reasons].' No, they couldn't do that. But it was a good slogan."

Cable laughed at the company's claims that it spared no expense in providing medical care when an accident occurred. "That sounds stupid," he said. "You know who the doctor was in first aid? Oh, Lord, he was a World War I veteran; he was a doctor in World War I. He was a butcher. He didn't operate on anybody or anything like that."[24]

The year after the *Carolina Mountaineer* published its account, H. W. Sullivan, vice-president of the International Brotherhood of Pulp Sulphite and Paper Mill Workers Union, came to town to investigate conditions in the mill. What he found supports Cable's version:

> I arrived in Canton July 24, and found that the mill needed an organization, wages are from fourteen cents per hour to 30 cents. The plant operates on the old 11 and 13 hours. In addition to this they are treated like slaves. When the company officials discovered I was in town they discharged every man who was found talking to me. They also made it impossible to hire a hall to hold a meeting. Being balked in my efforts to find a meeting place, I left and returned to Asheville where I met with the Secretary of the State Federation of Labor and had an interesting talk with him. By the way, I think that after we finish spreading "democracy to the world" over in Europe, it might be a good idea to spread a little of it in Canton, N. Carolina, U.S.A.[25]

Sullivan had traveled by train from Washington, D.C., to Canton, probably at the request of workers interested in organizing. His impressions suggest that the Champion family and the safety first program fell far short of Robertson's ideals. Nevertheless, public relations and Robertson's reputation as a "good guy" constrained efforts to organize. Haney described the plant manager's influence on organizing efforts: "A lot of the old-timers were good friends of [Robertson's]. He talked to the people. He'd come to the mill and they related to him. And so they felt like it was a slap in the face toward the Robertson family to organize this place or who managed the place. To have a union was just a slap in the face to them."[26]

But there was a downside to working under a patriarch. While acknowledging that he "had the utmost respect for the man," Haney felt that Champion, under Robertson's leadership, "paid the individual and not the job. And the unions tried to protect the job instead of an individual, as far as wages. If I'm doing the same work as another man I should be drawing the same pay. But Champion would have never done that. They paid individuals. If somebody did a good job, they gave them a little bit more money than the next one." Robertson's policy of rewarding individuals with pay and privilege amounted to what Haney called a "favored child" approach. Workers sometimes responded to Robertson's approach with their own public relations campaign. "It led to what I'd call brown-nosing," Haney chuckled.[27]

In the early 1920s, though, "cooperative goodwill" successfully thwarted attempts to unionize the mill. Toward the end of his life, Robertson justifiably claimed credit for a number of technical "firsts" in the paper industry: the use of chestnut chips to reduce costs of wood supply, recovery of waste liquors, and the wheeler cell, which made for more efficient use of energy. He also wanted credit as a benevolent industrialist, creator of the model company town that met all the needs of its worker-citizens. In preparing his memoirs, he wrote:

> In the field of security for workers, Champion pioneered in establishing one of the first, if not *the* first, safety committee in the paper industry; was the first to replace two shift operation by three shift operation in *an* extract plant, and was among the first half dozen in the paper industry to follow this progressive prac-

ice. Champion, alone, provided what the workers called an "old age bonus," by which pay was increased 5% every five years up to a total of twenty five years. . . . Its old timer club meetings were new in the industry, and helped substantially in creating loyalty and good will between management and men. A credit union provided funds for emergency needs at modest cost and has proven to be an outstanding success. Champion's encouragement of home ownership by employees through long term, low interest bearing loans, helped, not only to stabilize employment, but also to make a more responsible citizenship.[28]

As Cable said, the safety committee often overlooked, or was powerless to change, hazardous conditions, such as the routine exposure to poisonous gasses. It is true that Champion experimented with the "progressive practice" of three-shift operation, which reduced hours and employed more workers. But neither this practice nor the comparatively good wages were standard policies until the workers fought a three-month-long lockout/strike.

In 1923 the always-volatile paper industry was struggling through an economic recession. Champion officials compensated by cutting some departments to part-time operation, trimming wages by 10 percent, and returning to two shifts. Some workers were ready to leave the Champion family's fold and contacted the American Federation of Labor. They formed two locals, one affiliated with the International Papermakers, the other with the Brotherhood of Pulp, Sulphite, and Papermakers. The locals elected officers and held regular meetings for several weeks while the company simply ignored their existence.[29]

This all changed abruptly in January of 1924, when Champion announced that the mill would close temporarily. Robertson was very careful in his public statements to blame the closing on market conditions, but most people, including the local press, believed this was only a front. E. Kaye Lanning has argued that the company simply saw an opportunity to break the union and ride out the faltering economy at the same time, believing that "workers with cold bodies, hungry stomachs, and no cash" would soon drop their demands for three shifts, no pay cuts, and union recognition.[30]

Unlike the 1960s, when merchants "were spreading rumors throughout the town that if you strike, we won't extend you any more credit," in 1924 the local community rallied behind the workers.[31] In the beginning, at least, the *Asheville Citizen* was openly in support of worker demands, and local merchants ignored the company's requests to deny credit.[32]

Charles Cable empathized with these early organizers. "*Union* was a bad word, and it still is in the South," he said. "People talked about 'outsiders' coming in and taking over."[33] Outside help came in the form of national representatives F. P. Barry of the International Papermakers Union and S. Ed Launer of the Brotherhood of Pulp, Sulphite, and Papermakers.[34] Cable believed that the later struggle for union recognition was successful because he and others were able to convince workers that "the union is us; it's not outsiders."[35] In 1924, however, the taint of the "outside agitator" still hung over organizing efforts. To people outside the mill, who had never worked the eleven- to thirteen-hour shifts, been exposed to toxic chemicals, or lived with the threat of having their pay suddenly cut by 10 percent, Robertson's famous "open door policy" looked like a warm and human approach to industrial relations. Barry and Launer, who were heading up organizing efforts and negotiations with company officials, were helpful to Champion's public relations efforts as the "outside agitators" trying to disrupt the harmonious relations. Perhaps for this reason the *Asheville Citizen*'s support began to wane and eventually swung full circle to support management's position.

In early February, with the company showing no signs of reopening the mill or negotiating with union officials, the union moved to seize the offensive. It called a strike and organized workers into picket lines. Now, at least officially, the workers were no longer waiting patiently for Champion to give them back their jobs; they were withholding their labor until conditions improved and their union was recognized. Robertson ignored the move and spoke as though he was still in control, saying only that as soon as economic conditions improved the plant would reopen and implying that the workers would return to run it.[36]

In fact, talks were being held between workers and company officials, although union representatives were conspicuously absent. An official from the U.S. Labor Department served as a mediator. The two sides agreed to a settlement that granted the workers two of their demands: three shifts and no wage cut. On the third issue, union recognition, the company wouldn't budge. Instead, it allowed for "committees of employees to confer with officials" when problems arose. The unions could still exist, although they would not be officially recognized by the company. Members would be rehired without prejudice.[37]

The issue of whether employees would be represented by their union or by a committee of "representatives" whose ultimate recourse was to appeal to the plant manager remained a sticking point. According to Cable, forty years later this committee, or "mill council," as it came to be called, was no more effective at representing worker interests than it was in 1924. "If you had a grievance through the mill council, which was really just a company [committee], the steps that you went through wound you up with the plant manager making the final decision. Well, that's no good. He's going to decide for the company, no matter what the grievance is. . . . They were always right, you see, you were wrong no matter what it was. In fact, in all the time I was on the mill council, I don't remember any grievance that we won. We took one all the way to the mill manager, and of course he agreed with the supervisors. He turned the grievance down."[38]

In their zeal to build their new union, and buoyed by winning two of their three demands, the returning workers began an intensive campaign to sign up their fellow workers.[39] Robertson got wind of a report that some were claiming the mill was to be a closed shop, with all employees required to join the union, and charged that this invalidated the entire agreement. "These actions I consider absolutely at variance and in conflict with the Open Shop plan as it was understood by me, and I believe by others present at the meeting," he told the *Asheville Citizen.*[40] Suddenly, union recognition became the focus, with the workers vowing to fight for it to the finish and the company determined to resume operations with a nonunion workforce.

The company made good on its two promises, dropping the wage cut and shift change plans while it strengthened its resolve to operate union free. In early March, it began importing replacement workers to fill the strikers' jobs and announced that it would begin production in two departments. The striking workers would be allowed to return to work provided that they turned in their union cards.[41] This fact so firmly stuck in the collective memory of the Canton workers that more than sixty years later Vanise Henson recalled with disgust that the company had "hauled in [scabs] in boxcars."[42]

Although there is no evidence of violence, this tactic must surely have heightened tensions on the picket lines. Someone, it is unclear who, contacted North Carolina governor Cameron Morrison requesting troops to keep order. Both local law enforcement and union officials were quick to comment publicly that no violence had occurred and none was expected, and so the threat of an occupying military force in Canton never materialized. The Canton mill resumed limited operations with a skeletal workforce comprised of imported replacements and a hundred or so former union members who chose to renounce their membership and cross the picket lines. This latter group grew as a particularly rough winter hung on. Lanning has reported that in the soda department and paper mills alone five hundred workers turned in union cards and crossed within a week and a half. By mid-March that number had doubled and by April the mill was operating at full scale.[43] Champion had won on the issue it felt most important, union recognition, but it was not a total victory. The workers had organized and protected their wages and hours. It would be decades and many struggles before they would have an officially recognized union, but these subsequent struggles drew strength from this early partial victory.

For the next twenty years, though, Robertson's strategy of cultivating "cooperative goodwill" stifled all efforts to organize a union in Canton. Events just five years after the 1924 strike, and just beyond North Carolina's Appalachian foothills, provide a contrast that illustrates how effective the strategy was. In the cotton mill villages of Gastonia and Marion, owners responded to falling markets with many of the same tactics that Champion had tried. They reduced wages, lengthened the workday, and tried to squeeze more production from workers using the same scientific management principles that Peter Thompson had tried and discarded at Champion in 1906. Southern textile workers dubbed these tactics the "stretch-out" system.

In Elizabethton, Tennessee, mill workers walked off the job and stayed out for three months. When the walkout spread to Gastonia, owners responded to worker demands for increased wages, a forty-hour workweek, and an end to the "stretch-out" by organizing a "Committee of One Hundred," a vigilante group whose purpose was to intimidate striking workers with threats and open acts of violence. The workers fought back, and this time North Carolina's governor did call out the National Guard, which proceeded to break up the picket lines with violent force. Gastonia's police chief, Orville Aderholt, was killed in an exchange of gunfire. Ella May,[44] a mill worker who inspired other workers with her original ballads and her courage to stand up to bosses, was shot in the throat and killed while on her way to a union rally by a group of men probably acting on behalf of the mill owners. The owners made few concessions and thoroughly crushed the 1929 strike.[45]

But the bitter memories of having their own state militia called into action against them, the ranting of the rabidly antiunion local newspaper, and the organized terror of the bosses' "Committee of One Hundred" smoldered. Earlier, in Canton, Reuben Robertson's words had sought a reconciliation, albeit on his terms: "The boys have a very fine record since the mill closed about six weeks ago and I have not felt at any time that they would be trouble. We are going to give them all the opportunity possible to return to work. The doors are by no means closed to any who want to return."[46] But in Gastonia, mill owners smugly believed they had crushed the union forevermore and had so intimidated the workers that they might never attempt to organize again.

They were surprised when, in 1934, textile workers, emboldened by New Deal legislation strengthening their right to organize and furious over still another attempt to ratchet up the stretch-out, responded to the United Textile Workers Union's call for a general strike. Approximately four hundred thousand mill hands across the South walked out in what has been called the nation's largest strike ever.[47] Reuben Robertson, just 120 miles away from Gastonia, had his beliefs confirmed. "Cooperative goodwill" was more effective than direct confrontation at curbing unionism.

The next effort to organize in Canton was ill-planned and doomed from the start. The year was 1946, and the issue this time was Champion's policy of guaranteeing veterans returning from World War II either the job they had left or a comparable one with no loss in seniority, a policy that complied with the GI Bill of Rights. A group of workers who stood to lose their jobs began holding meetings, electing officers, and pushing for a certification election. The strategy of organizing around such an issue proved disastrous in the patriotic fervor of post–World War II. As Charles Cable said, "nobody in the plant would pile up around a bunch of people like that. Everybody in the plant was patriotic." The effort died before it came to a vote.[48]

In the early 1960s, Champion responded to a sudden drop in the paper market by limiting raises to half cents or quarter cents and laying off workers.[49] Since the organized resistance of 1924, Champion workers had, for the most part, accepted the company's claims that such measures were in their own best interest. As Doug Gibson explained, even after they had a union, its members were keenly interested in the economic health of the company: "You have your years of lean times, and you have your feasts. But all in all, the union has been very supportive of the company, trying to keep the company going strong. Because it's our jobs that we're protecting when we do that. And our community. So you have to see that the company's in a strong position." This perspective is tempered, though, with a strong commitment to traditional union values. Gibson continues, "But then, on the other hand, you want the employees to be taken care of and looked after the way they should be. So it's a delicate role that you have to play in that."[50]

Robertson's "cooperative goodwill" continued to reinforce loyalty to the Champion family, even among those who had lost their jobs. Jack Chapman, an in-plant leader in the union drives of the 1960s, described how Robertson treated one laid-off employee: "I knew a man that was laid off for a year. There was a company store, and Mr. Robertson told [the employee's] wife to buy anything they needed and put it on the bill, and when he came back to work he could pay it back a little at a time."[51] Reuben Robertson Jr., who had taken over for his father in the early 1960s, continued the cooperative goodwill policies. However, the Robertson era, and the Robertson philosophy, came to an abrupt end when the son was struck and killed by a car in the streets of Cincinnati.

John Scroggs had moved to Canton from nearby Clay County in 1958. He described the sudden change in managerial style in the early

1960s: "In my view [Robertson Jr.] was carrying on all his dad's philoso-
phies, trying to take care of the people and so forth. In this difficult
time he had brought on a man named Carl Bendetson. They had met
while Robertson was assistant secretary of defense and Carl worked for
him. Carl started cutting and slashing like some corporate raiders do
now, searching for the bottom line. So employment dropped about a
thousand in a couple of years. It dropped from like 3,300 to 2,300."
Still, Scroggs and others understood Champion's position. He
explained that "it was the manner in which it was done" that got the
workers talking about organizing a union again. "They made reductions in the workforce in different ways. And the first, as I recall, was
'undesirables,' people with bad attendance records. . . . And then they
did some [layoffs], more or less, by seniority." Scroggs spoke from
experience as he described the effect of the "corporate raiders" on the
Champion family.

> I might as well tell you this; it's what made a union man out of
> me. . . . There was a fellow named Willard Haney who worked in
> what we call fire control. He was very active in organizing and
> they cut that crew and moved him back to the pipe fitter crew.
> He and a guy named Hugh Allen sort of headed up [organizing
> efforts]. They moved Haney back to the pipe crew as a helper. I
> was in the pipe fitter crew, and, . . . [they] were pretty active in
> the organizing meetings. I attended some of those and went
> along and carried others in my vehicle. [So the decision was
> made] that they were going to do away with all the pipe fitters,
> helpers and apprentices. They got me and two other apprentices
> and several helpers. I feel like I was a victim of them getting
> Willard Haney. I can't prove it, but I know that's what happened.
> So we went back into the transfer pool and so forth. . . . Willard
> could see the handwriting on the wall. He had, supposedly, a
> weak back. . . . They put us on those lifting jobs and Willard found
> a job in another plant. . . . So, in my opinion, they accomplished
> what they wanted to.[52]

Whether or not the new management at Champion was using such
classic union-busting techniques, it is significant that Scroggs and
others believed they were. Their loyalty to a company whose president
had routinely visited them in their workplaces was slipping away. In

its place a suspicion was growing that they were now working for a company that would use every trick at its disposal to crush their efforts to protect their jobs. According to Chapman, there were other motivations to organize as well. "In four years, we only got four cents in pay raises. We were never told what the company's financial status was. Everything was secret."[53]

But old habits, and long-held loyalties, die slowly. The first few certification elections were landslide victories for the company. "We had about three elections in a short period of time in the early '60s," Scroggs remembered. "[There's a] story about the number on the steam engine, 2104. . . . That was the number for the company. . . . twenty-one hundred and four had voted against the union."[54] In the Canton mill such a number represented a near unanimous rejection of the union.

Not all of the company's tactics in the early 1960s were as subtle as transferring organizers to one crew and then abolishing the crew. At the same time that it blocked union leaders from access to local meeting rooms, the company held "captive meetings" at a local movie theater. At these mandatory meetings, held during normal working hours, company officials described the inevitable problems that the union would bring to their peaceful lives. Time and again they trotted out the notion of the Champion family, whose primary concern was the welfare of its employees. Scroggs remembered that Bill Lehmkuhl, vice-president and division manager of the Canton and Waynesville mills, tried especially hard to pull at the workers' heart strings: "I remember one election, they brought us over to the old Colonial Theater and [Lehmkuhl] got up and talked to us. They'd take us like, maybe a couple hundred at a time, and they'd fill the theater to talk to us. We called Lehmkuhl 'the actor.' I remember him saying, 'If I've ever hurt anybody, I'm sorry,' and tears in his eyes, you know." Lehmkuhl also was known for emulating Reuben Robertson Sr.'s personable style. But because he lacked Robertson's talent for remembering intimate details about the workers, he needed help: "Lehmkuhl had this guy that was editor of the *Chips* [company newsletter], now I'd rather not call his name. But they'd go around through the mill, and this guy knew practically everybody. So I think what he did, he'd

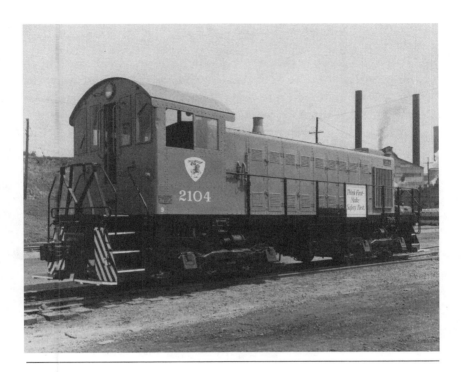

Locomotive 2104, whose number represented the votes cast against union representation in an early 1960s election. *Courtesy of the Snug Harbor Photo Archives, Canton. Reprinted with permission.*

tell Mr. Lehmkuhl, 'that's ol' John Scroggs; he's got two kids,' and so forth, give him a little history on you. And then Bill would come up, 'John, how's the kids?'"[55]

Champion's managers weren't content merely to copy Robertson's style. They were also known to call on the grand old patriarch himself in the days before union elections. "I remember them bringing him back before one union election. He went through the mill in a golf cart. ... And they took him through the mill to campaign against the union," Scroggs said.[56] Charles Cable remembered that the sight of Robertson, close to eighty years old at the time, being chauffeured around the plant in a golf cart had an unintended effect. Instead of stirring up employee loyalties to the company, such tactics increased the growing resentment.

"They used him [Robertson]," said Cable. "He was a swell person and I loved him."[57]

Dan K. Moore, who would eventually become governor of North Carolina, also played a part in the company's antiunion campaign. Moore was born in Asheville, just twenty miles down the road from Canton. After graduating from law school, he returned to western North Carolina to start a practice. Following a stint as a state legislator and service in World War II, Moore was appointed a superior court judge by Gov. R. Gregg Cherry and served in this capacity until 1958. He then resigned his judgeship to accept a position as divisional counsel and later assistant secretary for Champion.[58] When Moore left Champion in 1964 to run for governor, the company jumped at the opportunity to have a sympathetic ear in the state's highest elective office. According to Cable, they saw contributions to Moore's campaign as a good investment: "Dan Moore ran for . . . the Democratic nomination for governor. And they had to have a runoff; he didn't win the nomination. . . . The company was banking him financially, 100 percent. So Bill Lehmkuhl went with him everywhere he went, financially. He won the second primary and then was elected governor. But the company financed it, Champion."[59]

One of John Scroggs's jobs in the early 1960s was watchman, or security guard, which required him "to chauffeur Mr. Moore around some, take him to meetings and this and that. I remember that Champion provided him with a big Buick to drive around."[60] But Moore is most remembered by the older Champion workers for preaching a "Bury the Union" mock funeral service while standing over an actual casket that had been paraded through the plant. State government and big industry in this right-to-work state were united, forming a seemingly impregnable barricade before the union organizers in Canton.

Ironically, Charles Cable, who probably did more than anyone else to organize the effort that finally succeeded, voted against the union in these early 1960s elections. He had worked as a supervisor and felt that "the company was good, but they were beginning to take things [benefits and privileges] away from us that we had had through the years." In spite of having been "reared in a family that was antiunion, 100 percent," and believing it for most of his life, Cable began listening to

In his latter years, Reuben Robertson (in the sport coat) was paraded through the mill in a golf cart to remind workers that the Champion family did not need a union. *Courtesy of the Snug Harbor Photo Archives, Canton. Reprinted with permission.*

"some boys that worked for me who worked for the union." They did not fit the stereotype of the union agitator that his family and the company described. Rather, "they were good fellows . . . . they were grade A, they weren't 'outsiders.' They weren't communists or anything like that. like the company painted all of them."[61]

Gradually, Cable began not only to see the need for a union but also to think about the most effective strategy for organizing one. "I got to looking at the situation differently," he said. "I said, 'fellows, you're going about this thing the wrong way. If we get the union in here we're not going to depend on those international representatives to come in here and organize and do all our visiting. . . . They

Left to right: North Carolina Governor Dan K. Moore, Champion executive Robert Longbine, and Reuben B. Robertson, c. 1964. *Courtesy of the Snug Harbor Photo Archives, Canton. Reprinted with permission.*

are outsiders and the company has already branded them as that. What you're going to have to do is get an in-plant committee made up of people in the plant. Let us organize; let us be the ones to do the visiting.'" Cable eventually shared these thoughts with the union's international representatives, who "came to visit me and we spent a whole afternoon together in my house . . . [and] they asked me if I would head up a committee like that." Now more certain than ever that "we did need a union because the company was taking things away from us and there was no right in the cause," Cable was still reluctant to be an active participant. "I told them, 'no, I wouldn't have anything to do with it.'" But Cable is a deeply religious man, an ordained Baptist minister who never makes important decisions without prayer. "If something did happen something had to happen drastically," he thought. "So I thought that over and prayed it over and I went up on the mountain. I had a big ol' dog and that dog and I spent a whole day together on top of that mountain. And I decided that that was the thing to do, that if I was going to be for it then [I would] get in there."[62]

Cable offered his services to union's international representatives on the condition that "we'll have to do it my way." He insisted on designing the literature himself, telling the union reps that "nobody's paying attention to your literature." Let the local people take the lead in organizing, he argued, because "[the company is] saying you're a bunch of communists and antichrists." The international representatives either saw the wisdom in Cable's proposal or they reasoned that they had nothing to lose because they had made no headway themselves. Cable now found himself in charge of the organizing campaign and "got a committee together and wrote all the letters to the employees during the campaign."[63]

After writing the letters Cable would have "the committee of about ten people . . . sign them . . . with me." The letters were designed to counter the company's charges that the union was just a group of outsiders trying to take over their lives and get a share of their wages. They stressed the need for the Canton workers to take control of their own lives and portrayed the new Champion management, headquartered far away in Connecticut, as the "outsiders."[64] "The time is at hand for us to make our decision," read one. "We cannot evade the responsibility of making the right decision for ourselves and the people who will work here long after we are gone. The Committee believes wholeheartedly with all the facts, we, as reasonable people, all 1,648 of us must vote YES for organizing together."[65] "They talked about 'outsiders' coming in and taking over, you know," Cable explained. "And of course the union was us, it's not outsiders. . . . We were people who had been there all our lives."[66]

Cable also tried to downplay the notion that organizing was a personal attack on the Robertson family and all they had done for Canton. While the company was outfitting Robertson with a chauffeured golf cart and sending him through the mill to make emotional appeals to the workers' sense of loyalty, and while one of its top lawyers stood on the mill floor lampooning the union in a mock funeral, Cable chose to appeal to the workers' common sense: "[I pointed out that] it was business. That you didn't go to the bank and borrow money as something negative. If you had to do it, it was a business thing, a business transaction. You signed, and they signed and you were still friends. To me the union was the same thing, when you had a contract with the company and both parties signed it in good faith. That doesn't mean that you're at war with one another. That means that you've got to work together and try to make this thing work."[67]

When it came time to hold organizing meetings, Cable and the organizing committee encountered the same problem that H. W. Sullivan had faced forty years earlier. Champion's influence was so pervasive that the doors of all public meeting places were closed to the union men: "We had to meet in Waynesville, at the Dayco union hall. They wouldn't let us meet anywhere in Canton. They wouldn't let us meet in the town hall. We had an armory there that I guess was a federal building, and we felt sure we could meet in that armory. So we approached the people in charge of it. 'No.' We had a YMCA, and they wouldn't let us meet there." And while Cable was confident that "this is America; they can't shoot you for joining a union," he did receive telephoned death threats late at night. "And I been called 'Judas.' I got one note with thirty pieces of silver solder . . . . and the note said, 'Judas sold Jesus for thirty pieces of silver; what did you charge?'"[68]

But Cable and the committee persisted, and gradually the notion that a union was not "a bunch of outsiders" but simply an organization of workers taking charge of their own interests began to take hold. For the first time, it appeared that the vote for union representation would be close. On election night in May of 1966, as the votes were being counted, Cable saw it as "stacking up fifty-fifty. It was going to be very close." As the tally was stacking up, one for the union, two for the company, two for the company, one for the union, Johnny Barnes, Champion's Industrial Relations Supervisor, was still confident that Canton would remain union free. Calling Cable aside, he said, "When this is over with, you'll wish you'd have never heard the word *union*." "But we did win the election . . . by a very small margin . . . and so I've always been proud of the word *union* and what it means, or what it meant to me," said Cable.

While victory in the representation election was hard won, it was only the first step in building a strong and effective union in Canton.

As a "right-to-work" state, North Carolina does not allow the closed shop, which would require all workers in the plant to join the union. Now that they had their union, the organizers still had to convince their fellow workers to join it. Those who had joined elected Cable president, and since no contract had been negotiated and no dues were being collected, he and others often paid operating expenses with their own money. "Although we had won the election, for those months that dragged by, the morale of people that had voted for the union was going down. 'Hey man, we got a union, when are we gonna get a contract?' they were saying. And I don't blame them. But they didn't understand what we were going through with it."[69]

What they were going through was intense negotiations with Champion, whose representatives were "dragging their feet" over the language in the contract. "Our main point was not so much the wages, . . . but it was the language in the contract," Cable remembered: "The company didn't have to go with the language that had to do with lay-off or promotion or anything else. And we felt like the senior qualified people were the ones that should be considered for promotions and in the event of a cutback [layoff] or anything, the senior people should be given priority."

Finally, after four months of negotiations the new local and the company agreed to terms. Nearly forty years later, Cable was still proud as he held up his copy of the contract. "This was our first contract. It's dated September 1, and we had won the election in May, so in my opinion the company dragged their feet through those months. Actually, I believe they were trying to discourage the employees from joining the union."

Local 507, its first contract in hand, would now have to recruit most of the workers in the plant to join; otherwise, the union would be nothing more than a minority voice with no real power. Many in the plant believed that this was and always would be the case. The union, they thought, would never be any more than the mill council that had been created in the settlement of the 1924 strike, for which the ultimate appeal was the plant manager. "We got a good grievance procedure, ending up with arbitration," said Cable. "But we still didn't have the number of union members that we needed to have the power that we needed." However, Cable and the other officers soon had an opportunity to show that the union could flex its muscles: "The company fired three over-the-road truck drivers for refusing to ride with a truck driver that they felt was unsafe. He had had several wrecks and had one wreck back here over the mountains, and it just tore the tractor-trailer all to pieces. And when they [the three fired drivers] would ride with him, there was a cab where they would sleep when he was driving. That cab was torn all to pieces. I mean, it was just shredded. So they were told to go to work with this man and they refused."

But the three men had planned their action. Before refusing to work in a hazardous situation, they had met with Cable. "I wrote them out a statement, what to say. Don't say anything but this statement right here, 'I respectfully refuse to ride with blank blank because of his unsafe attitude. And I fear for my life if I do ride with him.' So the company wanted to charge me with conspiracy. I said, 'No, these are individuals. I'm not the author of anything legally, except I wrote the note for them to read to you.'"

Cable was not surprised at the firings; in fact, he had planned the next move. "We took it to arbitration. Now I handled the arbitration case because I was not only the president, but I was the business agent also. So I handled arbitration cases and grievances and everything else." The case had the attention of the entire Canton and Waynesville workforce, most of whom believed that the three fired workers didn't have a chance. The three had flatly refused to carry out an assignment, and although most still saw Champion as a good company to work for, it was one in which the boss held ultimate authority. "But we won that case. Got those three their jobs back and back pay." The effect of the victory was electrifying. "That's what made the union, that one arbitration case. Immediately, we had 1,800 members, just almost overnight. They saw that it really was what they had to have for protection."[70]

Champion workers had won the fight that their grandfathers had begun on the picket lines in the harsh winter of 1924. They were union.

CHAPTER 3

Local 507's Alternative

Champion's CEO had tempered his language and was no longer publicly referring to the Canton and Waynesville mills as "non-strategic facilities" but as "good, productive assets." Olson hinted that one of the industry giants, such as International Paper or Weyerhaeuser, might purchase them and "achieve synergies by integrating them into their existing operations."[1]

At Local 507, such statements fueled Alton Higgins's fears that a "bottom-feeder" might snatch up the Canton mill at a bargain rate and refuse to deal with the union. He recalled an earlier conversation with Jack Chapman, who was researching employee buyouts. Higgins was sitting in the union hall with L. J. Rose, the union's international representative, "kicking around every aspect, kind of brainstorming and philosophizing on what might happen, could happen. And I mentioned to L.J., 'Well, I guess the employees could buy the mill if we had to . . . if worse came to worst.'" Rose commented, "That's not too far-fetched." The response caught Higgins off guard. "I said it in kind of a kidding, halfhearted fashion. And the good thing about L.J. is he would follow up on something like that. And he did."[2]

Higgins was not the only Local 507 member who had thought about buying the mill. Richard Haney said that as soon the sale was announced, "[an employee buyout] was my first thought, it really was. . . . I mean, I didn't know the terminology, 'ESOP.' I knew about employee ownership, because Lowe's and some of the other places, Harris-Teeter, I knew were employee owned. How they went about it I didn't know. I had never known. And I'd never been interested in it." But he was now. Like Henson, Haney did not want to wait for a "savior [to] ride in on a white horse" to save the mills. He was ready to act in his own behalf.[3]

Rose had already considered the possibility of the union's buying the mills. He had received a letter from Frank T. Adams, founder and president of the Southern Appalachian Center for Cooperative

Ownership Inc. (SACCO), in nearby Asheville, asking him to meet and discuss the idea. Rose was definitely interested but was cautious enough to ask Bob Smith, a vice-president of the Paper, Allied-Industrial, Chemical & Energy Workers (PACE) Union to "check this Frank Adams out . . . and get back to me." Three days later, on October 27, Rose called Adams and arranged for a meeting on Thursday, October 30, at the Hot Shot Café in Asheville. Adams, Local 507's president Mike Coleman, and Rose would be at the meeting.[4]

Rose's background check of Adams revealed a man with a lifelong commitment to creating a just society. Adams authored the book *Unearthing Seeds of Fire,* an account of the Highlander Center in east Tennessee, where education is a hands-on activity aimed at creating social change. He briefly served as director of Highlander, and after leaving he began organizing worker-owned cooperatives, mostly in the wake of textile plant closings in eastern North Carolina and elsewhere in the South. He continued that work and branched out into employee stock ownership plan (ESOP) buyouts with the ICA Group in Boston, Massachusetts. Adams had spent the next eleven years organizing workers throughout the country to form ESOPs, often in partnership with local and international union leaders. By the time he contacted L. J. Rose, Adams had become one of the country's foremost authorities on worker-owned cooperatives.

Adams considered his efforts with Local 507 to be as much educational as entrepreneurial. In the introduction to *Unearthing Seeds of Fire,* he describes education as a process that "fosters individual growth and social change, nourishes the fundamental values, [and provides] complete personal liberty."[5] Still, Adams speaks carefully when describing himself as an "educator," making clear that he is first and foremost a "learner." "I make that distinction," he says, "because every business situation is different. . . . The workers always have a distinctly different history. The culture is different. The dynamic caused by the nature of the work—its hours, its routines, the attitudes of supervisors—always are different. I have to learn how to listen within that situation. And if I teach anything, in the usual sense of that word, it is how to learn. How to put the collective wisdom of a union local or an unorganized workforce to use as owners, not employees."[6]

Adams saw a number of positive factors at work in Canton. For one, paper workers have a long-standing respect in Haywood County. Doug Gibson remembered a time "years ago" when "you could ask anyone, 'Who do you work for?' 'I work for Champion,' they were proud to say that."[7] Also, their union had been won through an in-plant effort led by locals, giving it a legacy of independent local control. Finally, seven years earlier, Champion itself had contributed when it implemented a team-concept approach to contract negotiations. The company subsequently failed to honor the spirit of its agreements, but a team-oriented workplace had the appeal of the old days at Champion, when relationships were characterized by trust and verbal agreements carried the authority of legal documents.

At the Hot Shot Café meeting, Rose asked a lot of questions, and Coleman, according to Adams, "hardly said a word but listened carefully to what L.J. and I said." Adams explained that it was absolutely essential for the buyout to have the full support of the local's executive board. He remembered that Coleman "never blinked but nodded his agreement."[8] Finally, Coleman did speak up. "There's been talk about a buyout," he said, "but we don't know what that would take." Adams was up front from the beginning. He told the two union men that the odds were against them. Not only did the state of North Carolina discourage unions by outlawing the closed shop, it had at times been openly hostile toward them.[9] It was currently luring companies to relocate in the state with promises of a union-free workforce. As Adams later recalled, "a buyout of this magnitude was not just an economic challenge but would be seen as a political act, too, if successful."[10]

The subject of financing came up, and once again Adams's reply was frank and direct. He had no promise of a financial backer; in fact, he had no banking contacts in North Carolina. He had talked with American Capital Strategies (ACS), a firm that specialized in employee buyouts, and had found them willing to explore the possibility of working with Local 507 on a buyout bid. But, beyond that, they would make no further commitment until they had talked with the international and stock analysts who were familiar with the paper industry.

Adams clarified his role in the process. He would serve as a consultant to the union. He offered his twenty-seven years of experience and qualifications and assured them that in all of that time he had worked only with unions and never with management. He named his fees and then asked Rose and Coleman if they had any more questions.[11]

Coleman and Rose were interested enough to invite Adams to meet with Local 507's executive board and international vice-president Bob Smith five days later to explain the proposal. Adams agreed and the meeting concluded. The morning before the November 4 meeting with the local's executive board, Rose called Bob Smith to update him. Smith said that he would not be able to make the meeting or the general membership meeting two days later. Rose asked about a tentative meeting that had been scheduled with ACS, the potential funder, which would take place if the executive board and general membership voted to pursue the plan. Smith answered that, yes, he would be at the meeting with the funders, and Rose said he would let him know the results of the executive board meeting.[12]

Rose, meanwhile, was swamped with inquiries from union members concerned about the implications of the Canton and Waynesville mills being sold. Would their pensions be honored by whoever bought the mills? What about grievances that the union had pending? Could they file a suit to hold Champion or the new owners accountable even after the sale? At this point employee ownership was just one of many possibilities; most assumed that another paper company would purchase the mills, and they were worried about protecting their hard-won rights under a new owner.

On the morning that Adams was to present the buyout plan to Local 507's executive board, Rose arrived at the union hall at 8:15 a.m. and immediately met with Coleman. Rose told the local's president that Smith, the international vice-president, had changed his schedule and would attend the general membership meeting when the buyout proposal was presented. The two then discussed several questions that had come up should the plan become a reality.

Rose had done some research on ACS, and at the executive board meeting that evening he introduced Adams and gave board members a handout he had prepared on the potential funder.[13] Haney, who had already thought of the possibility of an employee buyout, was at this meeting as an officer in the local. He was hopeful from the beginning but as a veteran of the 1966 union drive, he knew that such a grand scheme would be successful only if the rank-and-file membership were firmly behind it. "I thought if we got started off right and if the union body as a whole supported it, we had a chance," he said.[14] Daniel Gregg, one of local 507's vice-presidents, was also favorably disposed. "I think we need to pursue or at least be looking at a possible employee buyout," he said.[15] Alton Higgins, who, like Haney, had already thought about the possibility of a buyout, was impressed when Adams "explained to us how it could be done, it had been done, and what it could mean."[16] The rest of the executive board was equally impressed. As Rose noted in his personal log, they "voted unanimously to retain the services of ACS and Frank Adams to start an employee buyout of the Champion Canton and Waynesville plants and all Dairy Paks."[17] "From that point on," Higgins later remembered, "we picked up that particular ball and ran with it."[18]

But even with the union's international representatives and the local's executive board behind the plan, it was still not a done deal. Local 507, after all, was born only after organizers turned the leadership over to local people who could act on their own, based on their knowledge of the local situation. In the same way that there had been skepticism in the early 1960s that a union could be beneficial for workers, there was skepticism now that a union could successfully buy out a large manufacturing plant and then operate it for a profit.

In addition to these doubts, many of the workers believed that Champion intended to operate the mills indefinitely, even if no potential buyer came forward. More than two years after Champion's announcement, Haney remarked: "People still don't believe it. I mean, you got people right now saying, 'if you guys hadn't done anything they'd have never sold it.' Or never shut it down. They were saying Champion never came out and said they'd shut it down. And that's the truth. They never did. They just said that they were going to sell, and that it was there. But not one time did they ever say that they were going to shut it down. And so people took that literally, that if nobody moves we're going to run right on."[19] But neither Haney nor Higgins believed this. And Doug Gibson had been watching Champion's corporate moves since the early 1990s, noting that they were spending less and less money to maintain and upgrade equipment and that people in higher management seemed less and less interested in the Canton operation. At least on some level, he had been expecting Champion to dump the Canton and Waynesville mills.[20]

While there was a good deal of skepticism among the rank and file, there was also a good deal of anger toward Champion. This anger had been mounting ever since the 1990 contract negotiations, when the workers had agreed to a nontraditional approach that was supposed to be built on mutual trust and understanding. The company hoped for a less binding contract. It argued that those who worked out the contract were the ones who would live with it, and so the workers and the managers should try to develop a mutual understanding as to how the contract would be interpreted. But, according to Haney, the process soon fell apart when Champion began moving out its managers.

> Two years after the negotiations, all of [the department managers] were gone. We were still there, but they weren't. And so they had new people and they would read the contract and they'd say, "I don't care what the intent is, this is what the language says." . . . That's not saying they weren't good people, but I didn't know them. And they were brought in here for one reason, and that was to cut people out, cut jobs out. . . . The way they went about it is what killed me. It was, "I'm the boss and this is the way it is. And if I want to cut it out we'll cut it out," rather than coming to the union and saying, "look, I think we need to do this." And thus establishing the ground rules.[21]

Feeling that the company had not lived up to its agreement and that management was becoming even more autocratic than it had been before, the workers resisted. "Grievances went through the roof," Gibson recalled. "It was just one thing after another. They were stacked up and they just kept stacking up."[22]

So on November 6, 1997, when the executive board recommended to the union's general membership that Local 507 explore the possibility of an employee buyout of Champion's Canton and Waynesville plants, Higgins noted that they were "tired of Champion's management style. The employee empowerment movement in participatory management . . . had been introduced and then immediately taken away and went back to a total autocratic management style."[23] And while some Champion workers refused to believe that the company would ever sell, others believed that something drastic would have to be done, and done in a hurry.

Vanise Henson remembered hearing of the plan at the general membership meeting. "I was more in favor of it than I was against it. I knew we were going to have to do something. I didn't want . . . an antiunion company coming in here and just shutting us down." Henson was also moved by the thought of what would happen if the mills did shut down. Two of his sisters and four brothers had worked for Champion, and his father had retired after thirty-four years service. He thought of the next generation and what would happen to them without the security of the high-wage manufacturing jobs the mills had provided: "I felt sorry for the younger people. I guess deep in my mind I really wanted to see something else happen [rather than the mills being shut down] that would solidify their future. You got young people that have twenty or thirty years left [until retirement]. I guess I thought more of them than I did myself."[24]

International Vice-President Bob Smith spent nearly an hour answering questions raised by the membership. Most concerned benefits and what could happen to them if the mills were sold. In addition to voting whether or not to proceed with the buyout and approve at least $100,000 of the union's funds to retain ACS, the local was electing officers on the same evening, and Coleman was facing a challenge from James Hutchinson.[25] When the vote was finally taken, the fear of losing the mills to a union-busting company, anger and mistrust of Champion, and a growing desire to take their destiny into their own hands combined to push the workers to an overwhelming approval of the plan to explore the buyout possibility. The final vote was 130 in favor and only 7 against.[26] The election of officers was closer. Mike Coleman, running for reelection as president, was forced into a runoff with James Hutchinson that he eventually lost.[27]

With full support of the local's executive board and the general membership, Rose and Adams turned their attention to the upcoming meeting with ACS.[28] They had no illusions about the importance of this meeting; it was the most critical so far. The supportive community, the long history of struggle for good wages and safe working conditions, the pride in being a third or forth generation Champion employee and in knowing that this meant being a part of the economic foundation of western North Carolina could all be lost if the buyout bid did not secure funding. Local 507 was stepping into the world of financial high rollers; it was indeed a gamble, but one that many felt was their only option. Daniel Gregg, for example, was thinking about how his grandfather had worked in logging in the early part of the century, felling the trees that Champion used to make its very first dollar in Canton. He remembered the struggles of all the Champion workers since then who had fought to bring the union, and he was moved by a fear of losing all this. He saw the buyout as a chance to "make a wrong into a right."[29]

The executive board's meeting with ACS representatives was scheduled for the morning of November 13. Three days before, Rose and Adams met to clarify some questions. Adams made sure that Rose had copies of *ESOPs: Unions and the Rank and File*, a shirt-pocket-sized booklet he coauthored with Gary B. Hansen, a labor economist and frequent adviser to the U.S. Department of Labor.[30] Adams had spoken with Adam Blumenthal and John Hoffmire of ACS, which, at the time, was among the few investment banking firms willing to invest in union-led buyouts. He told Rose that Blumenthal had asked for a tour of the plant and a meeting with the plant manager. He also told Rose that due to the size and scope of a buyout of the Canton and Waynesville mills, ACS might have to seek an additional investor and ask the union to underwrite some of the expenses. Adams, however, felt that the union should not have to come up with this money and suggested that they contact the local Economic Development Authority for financial support.

Adams then asked if Rose would mind if he brought Chris Just, a new SACCO associate, along to the meeting "as a learning experience for him." At the time, Just was director of the Mountain Microenterprise Fund, an organization that helped individual entrepreneurs start or expand their own businesses. Adams stressed that there would be no extra charge to the union for Just's involvement, and Rose replied that this was fine with him.[31] Later that evening, after checking with company officials, Rose called Adams back and told him that he would probably be unable to arrange the tour of the plant for Blumenthal. The company claimed that there could be legal problems with showing preference to a bidder, and giving ACS a tour this early in the process might be seen as giving inside information to the union's bid.[32] Rose and Adams may have been encouraged that the company was taking the union's bid seriously, but Adams agreed that a tour might cause legal problems later on.

On November 13, Rose picked up Bob Smith at his motel and took him to an early morning executive board meeting at Local 507's union hall. The first thing Adams noticed was that the local's president he was meeting with on November 13 was not the same one he had met with two weeks earlier at the Hot Shot Café. He had not been aware that a contested election was pending and wondered if his plea for firm support from the executive board and the president in particular had been heard. He remembered that Mike Coleman had officially presided at the November 4 general membership meeting but that Rose had done most of the talking. Now it was James Hutchinson who sat across the table from the ACS representatives as president-elect of the union, and Adams began to wonder whether or not the union, and therefore SACCO, was adequately prepared for this crucial meeting.[33] His concerns about Hutchinson, who had served as a vice-president and had considerable experience negotiating contracts, would soon be put to rest.

ACS had sent two representatives, one of whom was Adam Blumenthal, a vice-chair of ACS's board of directors. The international union was represented by its vice-president, Bob Smith, and Rose Local 507's entire executive board, along with Steve Wells and Mike Ferguson, recently elected vice-presidents, were present. Kenny Sutton, who was chair of the local's benefit committee, was also present, a fact that Rose was unhappy with. He later came to believe that Sutton had invited himself and that Doug Holland, an executive vice-president, had reluctantly agreed. Rose noted that he "had strong reservations about Kenny being there . . . as he was not a board member, and this was a special called board meeting."[34]

Blumenthal opened the meeting by giving a history of ACS and its accomplishments, focusing on two successful employee buyouts. He then went through the steps typically involved in a buyout and explained how the funding was usually handled. Moving on to issues of corporate structure, he described several possible models for management and boards of directors.[35] Adams sat quietly through most of this, pleased that the union members responded with a barrage of questions. In spite of what he had noticed was a rather rigid hierarchy within the union, these were individuals who demanded all of the facts before acting. They would likely work well with Adams, who wanted the process to be democratic from the start, with the local out front making the decisions and SACCO quietly providing information, helping to arrange contacts and lending support from behind the scenes.[36]

At around noon Rose and Smith excused themselves from the meeting to get Smith on his flight home. When Rose returned, the ACS representatives had departed, and he met with the executive board to decide whether or not to proceed with the buyout in light of what they had learned. Sutton voiced a lot of opinions at the afternoon meeting, and Rose found it harder and harder to keep silent.[37] For most of the union men present, this was just Kenny being Kenny. As Sutton says of himself, "I've always been very vocal, and most people either like me or they just fucking hate me. . . . I'm not a very passive person. If I think it sucks, I'll say it sucks. If I think it's good, I'll say it's good."[38] Rose never claimed to "just fucking hate" Sutton, but he did become more and more irritated at what he saw as an attempt to dominate. At one point, Sutton seconded a motion and Rose "called the board's hand." He "told them that this was an executive board meeting and that the board was the only one to make or second motions." He argued that there could be legal problems later on if nonboard members participated in these high-level decisions. The other union men, whom Adams described as meticulously attentive to the official union hierarchy, deferred to their international representative. Rose was not at all satisfied that Sutton had been sufficiently reigned in. Later that evening he made a foreboding observation in his personal log. "I am sure that we will hear more from this before it is over," he wrote.[39]

Finally, the board agreed that Local 507 should pursue the buyout of the Canton and Waynesville plants and all seven Dairy Paks. It elected a six-person ESOP Committee to lead the process. Alton Higgins, a first-generation Champion employee with more than twenty years' experience at Champion, was elected chair.[40] The choice was a wise one. Higgins had a keen understanding of both paper production and humanity. As he said, "Having been in virtually every department, every group in the mill, at some time or the other and having seen how management treated the employees on the floor, that was probably what started piquing my interest in helping represent the individuals."[41] As the local's recording secretary, he had access to the executive board. He also had a reputation among the rank and file as one who was absolutely reliable and, although quiet, not the least bit shy about speaking out for a worker who was being treated unfairly.

Doug Gibson, with more than twenty-six years' experience in the company, eighteen of them as an active unionist, was also elected to the committee. Gibson's family roots ran deep in Champion. His father had worked until retirement for the company, and his brother was employed at Champion's Hamilton, Ohio, plant. He accepted the challenge because he was thinking of these roots and his desire to preserve them for the future through his son or daughter. "When they get old enough to go into the workforce," he later said, "I'd love for them to have an opportunity to put in for a job over here and live somewhere close."[42]

Daniel Gregg, who also brought more than twenty years' experience in various parts of the Canton mill, could trace his roots in Canton to a time when the mill was still a dream of Reuben Robertson. "My great-grandfather worked in the timber part of Champion, bringing what the mill needed in those early years down to the mill." Robertson had chosen Haywood County partly due to its abundance of timber, which he would need for pulp, and Gregg's great-grandfather had brought the first of it to him. "My two grandfathers worked here on various jobs, essentially maintenance work. And my dad, he had forty-seven years' experience in shift repair. And I've had twenty-three years so far." Gregg committed to the ESOP Committee because this was just simply too much to lose without a fight. "I didn't want to have to walk away from a lot of my family roots here," he said.[43]

Richard Haney, with more than forty years' experience, was a third-generation Champion employee. Both his grandfather and father had worked for the company for more than twenty-five years, as had three brothers, one of whom had worked to retirement. Like Gregg, he did not want to see this line broken. "I've got three children of my own and two stepchildren," he said. "My stepdaughter has got a degree in college and she went and interviewed for a job this week [at the Canton mill]. She's always had jobs, but she decided now she'd put in, and she passed the test and had an interview Monday. . . . And my son is thinking about putting in an application. So if neither one of them gets on, then my generation ends. But, you know, as long as you've got that opportunity, that's what counts."[44] Haney could trace his union experience back to the founding of Local 507. His name is on the charter that still hangs in the union hall.

Vanise Henson, who had been skeptical of the employee buyout at first but had come to see it as a viable option and finally as the best option, was also elected. Like most of the others, Henson came from a Champion family. His father had worked thirty-four years for Champion, and six of his siblings had worked for the company. He feared the layoffs that might happen if someone other than the workers bought the company. "Any time an organization buys out somebody else or merges, a bunch of people are going to lose their jobs," he said. "We knew that right off the bat. Then Frank [Adams] came in and he explained that we could buy this place. With some help we could just about write our own contract and have it approved by whoever helps us. And we could put whatever we wanted to in that contract. But the main thing was that we could do it differently than these merged companies or diverse companies, that we could go in there and do it through attrition instead of just throwing them on the streets."[45] Henson accepted the challenge to keep his coworkers in their jobs and off the streets.

The sixth member elected to the ESOP Committee was a cause for concern to Rose. Still bothered by Kenny Sutton attending the executive board meeting when he was not a board member and trying to dominate at times, he noted in his personal log that "the bad part is that Kenny was elected as one of the six-man committee."[46]

Sutton resents Rose's implication that he somehow wormed his way onto the committee. "Mike Coleman [Local 507's president] invited me to come to the meeting," he later said. "I was asked to come to that meeting and was elected from that group of people. It wasn't that I held my hand up and said, 'I want to be on this committee,' because you couldn't do that. It was an elected group, and I got the second most votes of anybody that was in there."[47]

One reason that Sutton wanted to serve on the committee was to preserve his own sanity. "Being able to be on this buyout committee was my only saving grace. I can imagine what I would have had to go through had I sat there for eighteen months . . . not know what's happening . . . I couldn't have stood it."[48] Without question, Sutton is the type of personality who has to be out front and vocal and in the thick of the action. Whether or not he saw the ESOP Committee as his ticket off the shop floor into management, as Adams later came to suspect, or whether he just simply could not bear sitting still while his fate rested with someone else, he brought a dominating, fiery, and colorful personality that at times would prove to be a liability and at others a blessing.

The stage was set. The players were about to embark on an eighteen-month struggle. Some would look back on the struggle and say that if only they had known they never would have tried it, but all would agree that it transformed their lives.

CHAPTER 4

The ESOP Committee's Education

On November 18, the ESOP Committee held its first official meeting, electing Higgins as chair and Sutton as vice-chair. Drawing on their considerable organizing skills, they began exploring ways to attract support from other labor bodies and the community at large. They discussed the most effective ways to communicate with employees at their own plants and at the Dairy Paks, the seven satellite plants that turned Canton and Waynesville paper into juice and milk cartons. They considered strategies for dealing with the local and regional press effectively. Haney, Gregg, and Henson agreed to attend the next meeting of Snug Harbor, a fraternity of retired Champion employees, to seek their support. Henson would contact the Haywood county commissioners to get a feel for the level of support they could expect from local government agencies. And in a bold political move, these employees of one of the most notorious air and water polluters in an industry renowned for polluting decided to hold discussions with local and national environmentalists. This would mark a truce in a battle that had raged since 1911, when the state of Tennessee first filed suit against Champion for polluting the Pigeon and French Broad rivers.[1]

This decision to hold discussions with environmentalists was an early indication that the buyout effort was something much more profound than a bunch of unionized workers thinking they knew more than their bosses. It was more innovative than anything Champion had ever considered, and it showed the fallacy of the common notion that factory workers should stick to manual labor, leaving the planning and strategizing to the people with MBAs at corporate headquarters.

Adams, who was present at this first ESOP Committee meeting as the union's hired consultant, described how the group came up with this plan. "What are our options here?" he asked committee members. According to Adams, the members "immediately identified Champion's environmental reputation as a question that investment bankers would raise." This response did not surprise Adams, who knew that the workers had more at stake than anyone. "They could lose their jobs if they couldn't provide an answer to that," he said. "The second question I raised was, given that, how do you think we could go about meeting with the environmentalists? Those that specialize in forest products, wood chips, those that are most opposed to the chip mills, when you're using seven hundred tons of wood chips a day, those that are concerned about the water quality issue . . . and those who were concerned about air quality."[2] Adams's questions resonated with the workers. Gregg immediately saw a natural affinity between workers and environmentalists who were "just wanting to protect what we do have."[3] "Environmental groups," said Higgins, "can relate to employees, where they can't relate to big business."[4]

The ESOP Committee's decision to reach out to environmentalists was more than just good political strategy; it was also based on personal, sometimes painful, experience. Doug Gibson remembered how he had watched, as a boy, when "Champion used to put barrels across the river to catch the three- and four-feet-thick foam going down the river, to bust it up."[5] Vanise Henson remembered a time in the 1950s and 1960s when "you could drive down the street in Canton at five o'clock in the evening and have to turn your headlights on. You couldn't hang your wash out on the line. If you did it would have black soot all over it."[6] Kenny Sutton bought a mountaintop piece of property that he landscapes with great pride. He is fiercely protective of the water and air that he and his fellow workers share with environmentalists. "I've got spring water that I pull from. It's about three hundred foot down the mountain here. And I'm terribly respectful of the animals that are all around."[7]

It was not the environmentalists, and certainly not the Champion executives, who had the clearest understanding of what was at stake. Only Champion's workers could fully appreciate the complexities of operating in an industry that produces a strong local economy, a product that nearly every human being in the world uses, and enough toxic byproducts to seriously threaten the lives of those who produce and use it. They felt this conflict as members of a community, and they felt it personally. "I've always felt pretty hypocritical," Sutton said. "I've always had an inside battle with myself. Here I'm working for probably the worst industry there is out there. You're damaging trees; you're putting air pollution in; you're wearing the water out; all those things that you think you'd like to be against. But that's actually the way you're making your living."[8]

Champion's workers stood to lose much more than a pristine wilderness recreation area. Abuse of the environment threatened their very lives. Adams described the terrible toll of working with toxins: "That ESOP Committee, during the two years [of the buyout process], had personal experiences with cancer. Now whether it was caused by the proximity of their lives to the mill or some other factor no one will ever know. But Richard Haney's son lost an eye and most of his cheekbone and part of his skull to bone cancer. . . . James Hutchinson's daughter nearly lost her life to lymphoma. . . . I mean . . . every day there was a report about one of the members of the old-timers club, died, cancer, died, cancer."[9] For Champion's workers, purity of air and water was nothing less than a matter of life and death.

In late November of 1997, most residents of Haywood and Buncombe counties were still unaware of Local 507's decision to try to purchase the mills. This meant that the ESOP Committee would have to move fast to build support in the local community and governmental agencies. Among the citizens of western North Carolina, the initial shock from Champion's bombshell gave way to fear and panic at the tremendous social, political, and economic implications of losing a $5 million annual payroll. Some, such as the *Asheville Citizen-Times,* supported Champion's workforce. "Whoever purchases the plant," it editorialized two days after the announcement, "should treat these workers well. They deserve it."[10] But community support was not unanimous. Haney recalled hearing comments such as, "those people are already making a bunch of money. Why should we help them?" Haney saw hope in the fact that these voices were a minority. "But then we heard those other people saying, 'look, we can't afford to lose those jobs, so help them.'"[11] The ESOP Committee chose to build on the positive impulses of the latter group.

Some community members who felt a deep kinship with the mill and its workers, who knew that it was the community's lifeblood and saw it as the only hope for the future, were having lunch at a local

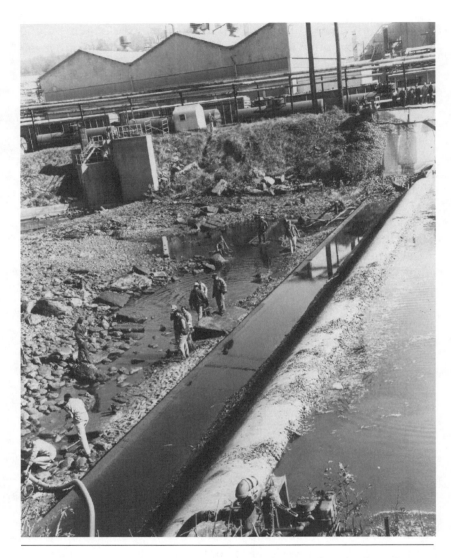

On the right is the dam on the Pigeon River built to regulate the flow of water into the plant. After a period of bad publicity about its environmental record, Champion sent out a labor crew to catch fish that spilled over the dam and toss them back upriver. *Courtesy of the Snug Harbor Photo Archives, Canton. Reprinted with permission.*

restaurant just after news of the sale became public. Waitress Sandra Hamby expressed their confusion and mixed emotions to a *Citizen-Times* reporter. "I don't think anybody's really sad or happy. They're surprised and shocked and unsure what the future will hold." Others at the restaurant that day were quick to blame the environmentalists who had pressured Champion to do something about the pollution of the Pigeon River. They were angry at their Tennessee neighbors and others who simply saw Champion, the Pigeon River, and Canton as "issues" and accused them of forcing the company's hand.[12] The corporate giant had always threatened to close or move when backed into a corner on environmental issues. Now many in Haywood County felt they had followed through on their threats, and they blamed these insensitive, meddling outsiders for what had happened. Clearly, building unified support from workers, environmentalists, government representatives, and others in the community would be a tremendous challenge for the ESOP Committee.

It was always possible that a new team of owners from the shop floor would become as aloof from everyday operations as Champion executives had been. Adams knew from experience that a change in workplace culture would occur only if the entire process were democratic from the beginning. If the new worker-owners had democratic input throughout the process they would grow to expect a democratic workplace when the buyout process was complete. For this reason, ESOP Committee members established a set of ground rules to ensure that they would operate democratically. At meetings, all committee members would be allowed to speak once before anyone would be allowed to speak a second time. They committed to trust and to maintaining confidentiality. They agreed that, in public, they would speak with one voice and that Higgins and Sutton, as chair and vice-chair, would be the official spokespersons. And, finally, they committed to educating themselves about ESOPs. They would study the material Adams had given them and insist that the outgoing local executive board do likewise.[13]

During the week before the ESOP Committee met again Higgins stayed in touch with Bob Smith, the union's regional vice-president. On November 25, the two discussed the pending contract with ACS and the international's role in the process. By this time Smith was openly supporting the effort and showed it by offering the services of Joyce Brooks, an AFL-CIO lawyer based in Charlotte. Another concern was how the ESOP Committee members would balance their work in the buyout effort with their duties on the shop floor and in the union hall. Higgins asked Smith if he could provide any help in getting release time from work during the buyout process, but Smith would not get involved in this, saying that it was a local issue. During this time, Higgins appraised the other ESOP Committee members of his discussions with Smith, honoring his commitment to proceed by group process.[14]

James Hutchinson, the newly elected local president, was invited to the second meeting so that he could be brought up to speed. Although Hutch, as he is known, had served as a departmental vice-president, Adams was still concerned. He had recognized early on that, while Local 507 was a strong and proud union where loyalty and solidarity ran high, it was also a local that marched to the step of the regional and international hierarchy. This was why he had stressed to Mike Coleman, the former president, that it was absolutely essential to have the full support of the local's president and its executive board. Adams had doubts as to whether a man just learning the ropes of holding union office could provide the kind of strong and visible leadership that would be necessary.[15]

At this second meeting, both Hutch and Coleman were given a copy of the minutes from the first and a copy of the pending contract with ACS. The committee then turned to the upcoming press conference, at which Local 507 would formally announce its plan to purchase the mills.[16] Everyone present knew the importance of this press conference. They knew that without strong support from the community, their local and state governments, the press, and other business and labor organizations their efforts would have little chance. This would be their first impression on the public. If they came across as poorly organized or incompetent, they might well lose out before the process began. If, on the other hand, they came across as knowledgeable and confident businesspeople who had done their research, they might attract the support of some who were sitting on the fence.

At one point during the meeting, Higgins left to talk on the phone with Smith, who said he would not be able to attend the press conference, another twist that must have concerned Adams. As he had tried to make clear, it could be damaging if it appeared that the international's support for Local 507 was lukewarm. It might cause potential investors to have doubts or cause the groups whose support they were trying to attract to hold back. Smith did say that he would contact other mills who had attempted or were attempting buyouts and would "share notes and ideas." He also agreed to fax the names of the local presidents who represented the seven Dairy Pak plants.[17]

The committee then turned to the strategies they had agreed to at the previous meeting. Higgins, Sutton, and Gregg would develop a generic letter to be faxed to local and state politicians, giving them information on the buyout plan and seeking their support. The committee approved letters that Higgins had composed to be sent to unions and worker organizations throughout the state and region. Timing was critical. Requests for support needed to be distributed shortly before the press conference so that when government and union representatives were contacted for comments they could speak knowledgably. And, finally, the committee approved the press release itself. It would go out just before December 6 and would announce to the world that the union was attempting to purchase Champion's two plants in Haywood County and possibly some of its liquid packaging plants.[18] It implied that the worker-owners would best Champion's recent performance in the market and its history of environmental degradation. "We know what it takes to make these two mills profitable," President Mike Coleman was quoted as saying. "We are determined to keep our jobs, and to run any mill we own with respect for people and the environment."[19]

The letters Higgins wrote to other unions, government officials, and community groups were similar to Charles Cable's earlier ones that had convinced employees that the drive for unionization was led not by "outsiders" but by local workers. To James Andrews, president of the North Carolina state AFL-CIO, Higgins described "the plight of Union brothers and sisters" in Haywood County who were fighting for "the goal of retaining jobs and financial security for Local 507." The letter requested "a letter of support, a call, a prayer, anything that would strengthen our journey down this unknown path." It concluded by appealing to Andrews's class consciousness, characterizing Champion

International as "unfeeling corporate mercenaries that have decided to boost their bottom-line revenues by the sale or perhaps the eventual closure of the Canton Mill."[20]

The letter to government officials was businesslike and focused on the need for help with funding. It mentioned that the union members were "waiting for a sales prospectus from Goldman Sachs, a New York investment firm hired by Champion to assess the value of the mills," and that they were "looking into the possibility of receiving some Economic Development funds." It asked politicians to "help us open doors with our efforts to raise funds to offset the high cost of consultant fees pertaining to the feasibility study" and requested a letter of support.[21]

Haney and Gibson appeared before the Western North Carolina Central Labor Council on December 1, five days before the press conference, and made a strong impression. As the council's president Larry Sorrells later wrote, "all in attendance were very impressed with the manner of the presentation and the remarkable job [the committee had] done in such a short period of time." Sorrells acknowledged the larger social and economic forces at work that Higgins had referred to in his letter. "With the trend of corporate greed on the rise," wrote Sorrells and secretary Laura Gordon, "we are afraid we will be seeing more of this short-sighted selling of profitable mills and plants that are the life blood of our communities all in the name of short term profits."[22] The letter closed with an offer to help in any way possible.

The following night, Tuesday, December 2, the executive board of Local 507 met, and the ESOP Committee was there to give an update of the buyout effort. After some deliberation, the board agreed to recommend that the general membership approve a plan to hire ACS and Adams as consultants. The board would also recommend that funds for the effort be allocated from the local treasury. Heeding Adams's advice to seek broad support, and perhaps remembering that the 1966 union drive had succeeded only after it received the support of the rank and file, the ESOP Committee stressed the need to keep the general membership informed throughout the process. The executive committee responded by proposing a series of four meetings between mill employees, family members, and a representative of ACS.[23]

Such attention to detail must have reassured Adams, who later explained that during a workplace transformation the workers must constantly stop and ask, "Are we going to take action and what are we going to do if that action succeeds and we gain our objectives?"[24] Adams had begun seeing the "Seeds of Fire" he wrote about in his book of the same name, where he defined education as something that "fosters individual growth and social change."[25]

In the next couple of days letters of support began arriving at the union hall. The local American Postal Workers Union pledged that it was "100% behind you in your efforts to buy out Champion" and encouraged Local 507 to "call us and we will be there to 'hit the street' or whatever it takes to support you."[26] Adam Blumenthal, executive vice-president of ACS, faxed a statement of support. In it he affirmed his company's commitment to working with Local 507 to pursue "an employee buyout for the purpose of preserving jobs and having a profitable business which can continue to be a mainstay of the Haywood County economy."[27] The following evening the executive board's motion to proceed with the buyout and fund it with Local 507's treasury was approved by the general membership, with 95 percent voting in favor.[28] For the moment, at least, the ESOP Committee was receiving the overwhelming support that Adams had hoped for.

On Thursday, December 4, the ESOP Committee distributed its first press release, and the following morning Waynesville's *Enterprise Mountaineer* officially announced that "Union wants to buy mill." The article gave only sketchy details of the plan and quoted one anonymous union member as saying, "If this happens, it will be the biggest employee buyout in the history of the nation," a claim that, while not factually accurate, did indicate a great deal of enthusiasm for the effort. Haney refused additional comment, saying only that details of the plan would come out at the press conference on the following day and in subsequent informational meetings. Champion refused all comment on the union's announcement.[29]

In all of the planning meetings and with this first public announcement, Adams remained discreetly behind the scenes, acting on his belief that a democratic workplace is possible only if the entire process is democratic from the start. "If you've done your job appropriately with that group of people," he explained, "they will have worked together democratically for six months to a year, or in some cases longer. And they will have the expectation that they're going to be able to continue to work that way in the future."[30]

So on Saturday, December 6, when these factory workers stood before the assembled press, invited government officials, and interested townspeople in their union hall to announce that they intended to purchase and operate the facilities of the largest corporate employer in western North Carolina, Adams stood quietly in the background. The public saw Higgins in a dark business suit and white shirt, his coal black shock of hair neatly combed back, revealing a ruggedly handsome face with a carefully trimmed moustache. He stood firmly behind a podium with the union's banner visible over his shoulder. While Higgins looked every bit the part of a forceful and knowledgeable CEO, the committee's co-chair, Sutton, stood to his right in faded jeans, his ponytail stretched tight and dangling down his back, his hands shoved into his pockets, looking a bit like a high-school senior forced to stick on a tie for portrait day. Higgins, always shrewdly aware of how appearance and approach might impact a particular group and thus the whole effort, had encouraged Sutton to add the tie. He later remembered, "I had a terrible time getting Kenny Sutton to wear a tie. . . . I wear a tie out of respect for the office, or if the group where we're going [expects you] to wear a tie and jacket. Once I brought an extra because Kenny is the world's worst for wearing tee-shirts or a shirt without a tie. And I brought him one and he was wearing a tee-shirt on that day, so that was a total waste."[31] Gibson and Haney stood in the background to Higgins's left, and outgoing local president Coleman stood off to the side on his right. The picture, which ran in the *Citizen-Times* and the *Enterprise Mountaineer* was a striking show of unity. It radiated confidence, determination, and the support of Higgins's comments by both the ESOP Committee and Local 507.[32]

In his opening statement, Higgins tried to allay the fears of the community and remind them of a past that many longed for. "Our goal is to save jobs and to give people a sense of security they have not had at Champion in a long time," he said. Coleman took his turn at the podium, confirming that the effort had the full support of the local. "We have been thinking about an employee buyout since October 8," he said. Characterizing Champion as the uncaring corporate entity opposed to the locals who were fighting for their community's survival, Coleman referred to the date as the day "Champion put our jobs up for sale." Sutton, who relished his reputation as unconventional and outspoken, stepped up to the microphone and stressed the need for action, for attempting to take control of their own and their community's destinies. "We feel this [buyout] is the only avenue we have as employees to have a say in our future," he said. He emphasized that their biggest fear was of "not doing anything." He then spoke of the business angle, surprising many skeptics with the amount of research he and the committee had already done and the insights they had gained. As if to assure the assembled that the union was not tilting at windmills but was embarking on a serious and well-planned business venture, he concluded by saying, "The demand for the product is there. If we didn't feel like we could have an avenue for the product, we wouldn't try to purchase the plants."[33]

In the days following the news conference, workers at the plant and residents of the town were suddenly being sought out for their opinions. Quinton Ellison, an *Asheville Citizen-Times* reporter, spent some time in Canton, hanging around on Main Street and trying to find out what the locals thought. At Skeeter's Park Street Café and Barbecue House, just across the street from the Canton mill, Sandra Hamby explained the importance of the mill to the community. "It may not be the greatest thing in the world, but it's all that we have," she said. "Everything is centered around it. They are also the biggest chunk of our taxes." "Champion is Canton," said another waitress at Skeeter's. "I worry about all the people that have been there for all those years. Lord knows I wish them all the luck in the world, but I don't want to see them lose more than they already have."[34]

Richard Haney took note of such comments; he sensed a change in the community's perceptions of Champion workers. As is common in times of crisis, people were beginning to put differences behind them, to rally together and seek common cause. "In the past, with Champion, you were sort of afraid to come out and say 'we're making good money' because people were jealous," Haney explained. "And in this area especially, because they felt like we made too much money for this area."[35] But in the days following the first press conference, a groundswell began to build. The voices of loyalty and support for Champion's workers were starting to drown out those earlier expressions of jealousy.

Support poured into the union hall in response to the ESOP Committee's letters. Local 507 had always had local clergy among its supporters; in fact, its very first president and its incoming president were both Baptist ministers. Now, the Reverend Roy Kilby offered his support, speculating that the union was guided by divine providence. "Perhaps it is God's will that the proposed buy-out of the company by the employees will be the answer," wrote Kilby. He said that if the plan were successful it "would indeed be a blessing to the residents of Canton, Haywood County and to the employees of Champion." To the Central Labor Council's vow to "hit the bricks" with Local 507, Reverend Kilby added a spiritual commitment. "We will be praying for those who will be leading in this endeavor and negotiating the details of the purchase . . . and, that God would grant you wisdom and insight in this very worthy cause."[36]

The next day a letter arrived from attorney David A. Craft of Asheville. Higgins had talked with Craft two days before, giving him background and details of the buyout plan and soliciting his help. Craft specialized in governmental affairs and was licensed to practice in both North Carolina and Washington, D.C. In addition to his numerous government contacts, Craft had friends in the investment field that he thought would be interested in financing an ESOP in western North Carolina.[37] Even early in the process Higgins was learning how to win the support of powerful legal and governmental people. It lay in something he called "just plain common sense," combined with diligent research. "We were naive enough, but yet thorough enough, to not be afraid of the political system, the political machine, if you will. . . . And we told these politicians, 'we're just factory workers . . . trying to protect our jobs, keep our jobs. Here's the economic impact. Here's the things that we found out. . . . This is what it means to 2,200 families. We need your help.' And we were so naive, apparently, that we were convincing."[38]

Apparently, Craft had sensed Higgins's determination, common sense, and commitment to the buyout plan. He was so enthused at the prospect of working with the ESOP Committee that he offered to help secure funding. And, perhaps most important, Craft agreed with the committee's assessment that it would need the support of government agencies and offered his considerable expertise in this regard. "While not an ESOP expert," he wrote, "I would welcome the chance to assist you in other related, but no less important, areas. A thorough government relations program at the federal and state levels could well be critical to your success." And to show that his offers were serious, he closed by offering "to come out to Canton and meet with you informally, and bring an investment friend or two."[39]

Other professional and influential people responded to the initial press conference, such as an Asheville psychologist, who wrote, "as a social scientist, I have some ideas that may be useful to you. I would be pleased to share them and if you think they are worthwhile, I would be pleased to work with the union to generate support and to prepare grant proposals to support local organizational efforts. I believe I can help you pull this off."[40]

But perhaps the most significant were the expressions of support such as that of Mr. and Mrs. F. M. Saunders of Waynesville, who wrote, "please do all you possibly can to not let the mill close. It would be awful for so many people to lose their jobs."[41] All six men on the ESOP Committee shared the Saunders' deep-seated concerns. They felt ties that went back three, four, and five generations with the communities of Canton and Waynesville, and they felt a tremendous responsibility to these people. They had long suspected, and now they knew for sure, that those in Champion's corporate headquarters did not see them as individuals, nor did they know their community and how it functioned. They felt they had been wronged by this faceless giant, and as Daniel Gregg said, "We as a committee had the desire to make a wrong a right."[42]

By all accounts, the first press conference had been a huge success. It had been less than two months since Champion had announced that it intended to sell the life blood of Haywood County, and in this time these six men, with the support of their local and international union, had organized, carried out careful research, and attracted the attention of government officials and financial backers. Champion's assessment that its Canton and Waynesville workforce was a "non-strategic asset" was beginning to seem rather premature.

CHAPTER 5

The River Is the Common Ground

One week after the press conference, Tennessee state officials agreed to drop their lawsuit against the state of North Carolina. The suit had been filed in response to the Environmental Protection Agency's approval of a variance that allowed Champion to exceed the emission standards of its discharge permit. Like most compromises, it brought an uneasy peace, leaving those at the extremes dissatisfied. Gay Webb, vice-president and founder of the Dead Pigeon River Council, had been critical of the proposed compromise when it was first announced, the day before Local 507's press conference, characterizing it as a political move on the part of Vice-President Al Gore.[1] But less than two weeks later, the Dead Pigeon River Council's president, Jerry Wilde, officially endorsed the agreement as "a step forward."[2]

At the other extreme, Canton resident Mary Stevens repeated the company's party line when she told a *Citizen-Times* reporter that the Tennessee politicians and the environmentalists were, "taking food out of our mouths" by threatening the mill's profitability. Stevens and others who had steadfastly supported Champion must have been shocked to see these environmental organizations so eager to compromise. Higgins explained the sudden change by saying, "We're opening up a dialog with environmental groups. We hope to both be able to accomplish and receive benefits to where both of us will be happy."[3] It was what Higgins would later call "a commonsense approach . . . just pure old what makes sense." Strategically, the commonsense approach had led to a series of meetings between Champion workers and representatives from the Sierra Club, the Dogwood Alliance, the North Carolina Clean Water Fund, and the Dead Pigeon River Council. But such common sense, which was the driving force behind the ESOP Committee's decisions, had never been Champion's approach in its ninety years in western North Carolina.[4]

When the mill first went on line in 1908 its impact on the Pigeon River stunned the locals. According to Richard A. Bartlett, author of

Troubled Waters, a book about the environmental controversies in this area, people along the banks of the Pigeon had lived in harmony with the river.[5] It was, for many, the primary source of water and food. Bartlett quotes Charles C. "Cromer" Chambers, who had lived on the Pigeon since his birth in 1887. Chambers remembered a river teeming with "sunfish, perch, bass, trout, hog suckers, horny ears, mullets."[6] But only one week after Champion's first discharge into the river, "there wasn't a fish in that river. That was the last you saw of them." He continued:

> It was terrible. When they first turned that water on it was as black as tar, and the suds [foam] were three feet deep all the way down that river. When they turned that dad gummed stuff in there they cleaned the fish out of the river. Got them in just one day. You could go to the branches [brooks] and creeks that empty into the Pigeon and there would be fish everywhere, stuck up trying to get a little clear water. Anywhere they could find clear water they were trying to get it. . . .
>
> That river turned just as black as molasses. Even the mud turtles couldn't live in that water. There used to be hundreds of those old muskrats and now there's none. People hollered awful about what they did to the river. They ruined all the swimming; everything. You couldn't go into the darn stuff at all.[7]

The stories that Cromer told were passed down through generations. When Doug Gibson and Vanise Henson were children they stood on the Pigeon's bank and looked at barrels strung across the river to break up the foam.[8] They saw their families' laundry turn dingy from the soot that hung heavy in the air.[9] They must have longed to swim and fish in the river as Cromer had. But as Cromer's memories of a pristine wilderness darkened with the water and the air, Gibson and Henson's hopes for financial stability brightened. A job at Champion promised a salary higher than many professionals in the area, family medical benefits, a home mortgage through the company-run credit union, and even college scholarships for employees' children. A stroll down main street through the air that was so dusty that cars had to burn their headlights would take them over sidewalks and along roads that Champion had paved, past the YMCA that

Champion had built for their families, and past the sewage and water-treatment plant that Champion had constructed. In spite of feeling "pretty hypocritical," as Kenny Sutton put it, "damaging trees, putting air pollution in, wearing the water out, all those things that you'd like to be against," the workers at Canton yielded to their love and duty to family and their longing to be stable providers of necessities and comforts, and they took the jobs that Champion offered.[10]

While they had chosen what seemed the best thing for their families, their community, and themselves, Champion's workers never completely severed their ancestral connections to the natural world, and they never completely resolved their own conflicts over what Champion was doing to their mountains. Kenny Sutton is a good case in point. He is quick witted and brash, with a history deeply embedded in Haywood County. In fact, while most people might be inclined to hide some aspects of this history, Sutton belts it out freely to anyone who will listen. "My step-granddaddy worked for Champion for years, retired from there," he begins and then follows with some slightly unsavory family stories that most would choose to leave in the closet. This strong sense of pride in his connection to the community and its colorful history is balanced by a deep, almost soulful love of nature. "I hate weeds and stuff growing in my gravel," he says pointing with pride to his neatly landscaped mountaintop home. "But I won't use Roundup, I won't use any kind of pesticide at all."[11]

"The employees that are living here and working here want as clean an environment as they can have," is the way Higgins summarized it. "But they want to keep their jobs also."[12] "We, the workers, were kind of caught in the middle," said Daniel Gregg. "We didn't like seeing the river the way it was, foam a foot thick and floating downstream." But up until the ESOP Committee led the drive for worker ownership, they had had little say in the matter. The battle was fought between Champion's corporate offices in Connecticut and environmental organizations and their allies in the Tennessee state government. "A lot of the hostility was from the corporate level," explained Gregg. Champion's attitude had been to "just dump it to the river and forget the air quality and all. We the workers kind of questioned some of that. The people in Tennessee were saying, "look, you know, we really need to clean this river up. And I think 90 percent of the workers here were pretty much in favor of that." The conflict facing the workers is evident in Gregg's next comment. "But not at the extent of losing what we had gained through the union and contracts."[13]

Eighty years of confrontations during which the adversaries and their positions changed hardly at all began building to a head in the mid-1980s. Until that time a cycle had repeated itself every five to ten years. Landowners downriver in Tennessee would begin to complain about the effect Champion's discharges had on the river. Champion would counter that it was working on the problem and would claim that it had already made great strides. When it suited the company's purposes, as when it faced a union contract negotiation or it wanted to cut production in response to slumping markets, it would plead poverty, claiming that the environmentalists and the state of Tennessee were harming its ability to make a profit. The company had perfected a process of whipping up fear among the workers and the townspeople by threatening to close the mill and then laying the blame at the feet of meddlesome environmentalists.[14]

The long war between Champion's corporate headquarters and Tennessee residents, in which government officials on both sides and various environmental organizations waded in as allies from time to time, is well documented by Bartlett. But the view from the shop floor in Canton is missing from this account. While Bartlett and others have found it easy to portray the Canton workers as "pawns" whom we should either chastise for their complicity or pity for their ignorance, the truth is that these workers were taking a careful and analytical perspective on the environmental issue.

In 1985 the North Carolina Division of Environmental Management issued Champion a permit that many felt left the company far too much wiggle room. Champion had begun a publicity campaign around its plans to bring a "state-of-the-art" filtration system online and did not expect North Carolina's permit to be seriously challenged.[15] The company was confident that its carefully crafted image of "good corporate citizen," an image that it had worked very hard to instill in its workers, would fend off any challenges. After all, it had even won the backing of Local 507. As Doug Gibson explained: "The union stood hand in hand with the company and tried to support the company because in doing so you're not only supporting the company but you're supporting the employees' futures and jobs in this area. Because if the company goes away, there's no need for the union. . . . So you have to go kind of hand in hand with them so that you can have the jobs for the people."[16]

When the Pigeon River Action Group (PRAG) and their allies in the Sierra Club and other environmental organizations decided to pressure the federal Environmental Protection Agency (EPA) to nullify North Carolina's permit and hold Champion to stricter standards, they accepted the official union position at face value. If they could have spoken with the union's rank-and-file membership, they would have discovered some unexpected allies. The environmentalists assumed that since, as Daniel Gregg put it, "Champion took a position of 'environmentalists are our enemy,'" the employees would be following the company line in lockstep.[17] In fact, the workers were ready to move toward constructive engagement with environmentalists. "We'd like to have clean water," said Richard Haney. "I'd like to see that river as clean below as it is above." Haney and other workers doubted Champion's claims that it could not clean up the discharge. "There is technology, but it costs," he said. "They can clean the water up tomorrow, you know. The process is there to get clean water."[18]

But the environmental coalition chose instead to confront Champion head-on by pressuring the EPA to override North Carolina's permit. In response to an EPA investigation, North Carolina did issue a tougher permit but did not require a specific number of "color-units," the measure typically used to gauge the amount of coloration in the water. The state of Tennessee, which by now was involved all the way to the governor's office, was demanding that the permit require a specific, and very low, level of color-units.

Another sticking point for the Tennessee citizens and their environmentalist allies was that if Champion failed to meet the requirements for one reason or another, the North Carolina permit gave the company an opportunity to hold a public hearing to present its case. Also, the Tennessee folks and the environmentalists were incensed at the way North Carolina officials had not issued the permit until the day before the deadline, consulting only with Champion officials. They saw this as blatant disregard for the well-being of the local people, another example of an international corporation with offices somewhere in Yankeeland buying off the local government and imposing its will on the people.[19] Although they were never actively courted by their fellow citizens in east Tennessee, "about 90 percent" of the workers inside the plant, according to Daniel Gregg, shared both the Tennesseans' desire to "clean this river up" and their distrust of Champion's corporate officers.[20]

In an unprecedented move, EPA responded to the pressure and did not accept the permit that North Carolina and Champion had been sure would settle things "for years to come." Instead, it ordered a set of public hearings on the matter—one to be held in Canton, North Carolina, and one in Tennessee.[21] Debate over the permit raged throughout the rest of 1985 and into 1986. Environmentalists focused on the number of color-units in the discharged Pigeon River water and how dark the water would be when it got to the Tennessee line. Champion continued to claim that it simply could not meet the standards that Tennessee wanted and that it would probably have to shut down the plant if it were forced to.[22] Gregg described how the company tried to beef up its threats. "Champion, at that time, offered the people here a chance to relocate. A lot did, and that was a good avenue for people who suspected maybe they would shut down here." But Gregg, a third-generation Champion employee, had seen these threats many times before and had learned to view them with skepticism. "It was a ploy, really, to justify to Champion's stockholders to go ahead and make this initial environmental improvement," he said.[23] In other words, the threats to close the mill were not just aimed at the workers; the company was also trying to convince its investors that they may have to bite the bullet and realize lower returns for a while.

Later, when Champion was forced to improve its environmental record as a result of these pressures, Gregg was pleased with the result. "You know, they were pressured to go ahead and put in the new pulp mill and the new BFR [Bleach Filtrate Recycle] process, but it has helped." Understanding the political pressures at work, he was also able to accept the impact the changes had on his job. "I've been

Lake Logan was constructed by Champion to increase the flow of the Pigeon River during dry seasons. In this photograph, taken in 1981, the lake has been almost completely released into the river. *Courtesy of the Snug Harbor Photo Archives, Canton. Reprinted with permission.*

pushed back to different jobs because of modernization, and I have to accept it," he said.[24]

The environmentalists gained a strong political boost in early 1986 when then-senator Albert Gore Jr. of Tennessee jumped into the fight. Gore, known as a political liberal and friend of the environmental movement, insisted that the EPA enforce a tougher permit immediately, one that specified strict color-units, because it was clear that North Carolina had no intention of revising its permit. Champion's response was predictable. It prepared to sue EPA and repeated its threats to slash production or close the plant if it were forced to comply with EPA's permit. EPA responded like a patient parent ignoring a childish tantrum, saying simply that it would submit a draft permit, hold public hearings, and then issue the permit. Champion proceeded with its lawsuit against EPA and then began a public relations campaign designed to reinforce its image of "good corporate citizen."[25]

The company's plan went awry when it had to announce that the ultrafiltration plant had not worked when it was tested. It refused to release results of the tests, leading opponents to charge that the company had simply discovered additional costs and had scrapped the plan because it would cut too deep into its profits. Champion did release a $200 million, five-year plan to reduce the coloration of the water. The hard-liners within the environmental movement, however, were unimpressed, claiming that it made no commitment to any measurable standard. Finally, Judge David Sentelle ruled, in response to Champion's suit, that EPA did have the authority to impose its permit, a development that stunned the company's corporate offices.[26] For the first time, the tried-and-true formula was faltering. The workers were questioning the company's hard line, and when the company tried to play hardball the courts ruled against it. EPA proceeded with its plans to hold two public hearings in May 1987, one in Canton and one in Newport, Tennessee. Champion, meanwhile, struck up its familiar refrain, making threats that it would have to close, hoping to scare the town and the workers into supporting it.

Some environmental activists began receiving threatening phone calls in a manner reminiscent of an earlier time when the company had fought unionization tooth and nail. One public schoolteacher was forced out of her job when she ignored her principal's request to have students write letters to the EPA in support of Champion. She chose, instead, to allow them to discuss the issues and write whatever they wanted.[27] And while the workers undoubtedly shared a sense of solidarity with Tennessee's citizens and were at times ashamed of their employer's antics, they were indeed "caught in the middle," as Gregg described it. "Workers are in a terrible bind today," explained Adams. "They have the real bosses to answer to and have to deal with fear at work on that level. But when an environmentalist group gets into the picture, they have to fear at work on another level."[28]

When the scheduled hearings were canceled, the more adamant environmentalists cried conspiracy, claiming EPA was stalling on behalf of Champion to give it more time to publicize its case. Others cited reported death threats made to PRAG and Dead Pigeon River Council members and agreed that a cooling-off period was a good idea.[29]

Champion took advantage of the delay. Through the summer and fall of 1987 it stuck by its claims that it was preparing to close the Canton plant if the EPA permit were forced on it. In early 1988, after EPA announced that two hearings would be held, one in Asheville and one in Knoxville, the company pulled out all the stops. It hired Price McNab, a noted public relations firm, to plead its case to the public, and it hired a transportation firm to transport Champion supporters to the hearings, moves that Gregg saw as a "corporation stand against the people of Tennessee."[30] Gregg and other workers also suspected that Champion was using its ongoing battle against the environmentalists, people who "are just, basically, like we are here," to weaken the union's bargaining position in an upcoming contract negotiation. "Of course, we were looking at ratification of a contract at that time," he said. "I knew that my concern was the same as what [the Tennessee citizens'] was and it was just a big ploy to get the contract ratified." Gregg had no interest in being bused around the region to serve as a pawn in the company's public relations campaign. He would refuse to attend the hearings because he "just wasn't on board with that mindset."[31]

Price McNab had developed a full-scale publicity blitz for Champion. The theme was built around the image of falling dominos, implying that if Champion were forced to close it would set a ripple effect in motion, which would eventually topple the entire economy of western North Carolina. The agency set up and ran phone banks, designed full-page ads, wrote and distributed television and radio spots, prepared form letters for citizens to mail to the EPA, and rented a warehouse in which it stored caps, buttons, bumper stickers, decals, banners, and signs with Champion's name and logo on them.[32]

In spite of this massive campaign, workers like Vanise Henson could muster only halfhearted support for their employer. "The employees knew that if they didn't get a permit their jobs were gone." But while believing that the company was perfectly capable of shutting down the mill if its profitability were threatened, Henson understood the complexity of the issues involved. "I can understand their [environmentalists'] problems. We need to do things differently to preserve what we've got. We can't just kill the Pigeon River. We can't just kill the mountains. Our future would be nothing without them." Henson knew, it was not "the employees' fight with these people; it was Champion['s]. Champion and them fought quite a bit."[33]

On the day of the first public hearing on the permit in Asheville, company-hired shuttle buses were sent to transport supporters from several points around Haywood County, including some public schools. Kenny Sutton, while having spent his entire working life at the Canton mill, was "amongst those people that didn't believe that we were doing all the right things with our environment." His fiercely independent nature recoiled at the company's efforts to move him about like a political pawn. Beyond this, an innate sense of fairness told him that it just wasn't "right to go down there and try to wear those people out."[34] He and others, such as Gregg and Haney, wanted no part of the pep rally Champion was organizing. The Asheville hearing lasted for eight hours, and by keeping the buses running throughout the process, the company was able to keep three or four thousand people, bedecked in Price McNab's yellow Champion hats and buttons, present at all times.

Some participants noted that every section seemed to have a carefully planted group leader who led cheers in support of the company's claims and hoots in opposition to its detractors.[35] So carefully scripted was Champion's presentation at the hearing that one worker who was recruited to speak later recalled, "I submitted a written document, you know, and said, 'This is my document.' I didn't speak as much as I was a presenter." When asked about the content of his presentation, the "presenter" laughed. "I don't remember. Oliver [Blackwell, the plant manager] probably wrote it."[36] In the words of Bartlett, "The citizenry of western North Carolina was subjected to a propaganda barrage that would have been the envy of Hitler's propaganda minister, Joseph Goebbels."[37]

Many who have commented on these proceedings have been blinded by the stereotype of the factory worker as ignorant, able to do only one small assembly line job, and incapable of understanding larger processes. For example, Bartlett's explanation of why so many workers went along with the company against the citizens of Tennessee includes the following: "The paper workers' ignorance of chemical processes played a part. Most have no chemical training. They work their eight-hour shifts in a massive factory, and, without an education in science, they cannot envision a system that would eliminate the tannins and toxic wastes and color and chemicals from the discharge. They might well think it is impossible. To them, Champion's statement that the color could not be removed was taken as holy writ. If Champion said it could not be done, then it could not be done."[38]

But later, when he was introduced to the idea of using a base other than wood chips for making paper, Richard Haney immediately saw the possibilities: "I agree with that; I'd like to see it happen. . . . I think you got a base here in North Carolina. As far as I know, hemp is illegal, but there is a hybrid hemp that is not. And with the tobacco industry the way they're going . . . that may be another industry for North Carolina. Instead of tobacco, have [the government subsidize] hemp or cane or whatever, because you can make paper out of a whole lot of those." In spite of having little formal "education in science," Haney not only understood the process when it was presented to him but also immediately put his mind to work planning how such a change might be tested at the mill. "Maybe try one machine on a different process and get a customer base already lined out. You've started a new trend." Haney, while possessing no "chemical training," also put in a good deal of thought on the chemical processes involved: "The process is there to get the clean water, but in doing that you've got to put more chemicals that take the wood fibers out, that you can't even see by the naked eye—that's what the color is. But in turn [the chemicals] cause more sludge." Haney was not content to give up as easily as Champion had. He continued to explore and probe for new and creative ways to solve this problem. "Maybe we could get a customer base that could use this sludge in paving roads, making block, brick, anything."[39] Hardly the words of a worker taking his employer's claims as "holy writ."

Although it was the "outsider" in the Knoxville hearing, Champion again attempted to dominate the proceedings. It offered workers a ride over on chartered buses and a box lunch to take along. Gov. Jim Martin led the caravan to the Tennessee state line in his limo. After Champion's speakers presented a brief version of the performance they had given in Asheville, the environmentalist side paraded its own experts up to the stage. They presented results of studies showing that the Pigeon was useless for fishing and recreation. For these reasons, they argued, the EPA should force Champion to accept the permit exactly as it was written.[40]

Most of the Tennessee state and local politicians who spoke were careful to stress to the workers present that they did not hold anything against them personally. They didn't want anyone in North Carolina to lose their jobs, they claimed. But they did not believe Champion's claims that it could not meet the permit standards. They believed it was possible to produce paper and profits (though probably lower ones) and clean up the river, a belief that was shared by some Champion workers.[41]

The Tennessee residents who spoke in Knoxville tried to emphasize their similarities to the Champion workers. The polluted river was destroying their economy, they argued. They emphasized the dioxin issue and related side effects such as higher cancer rates much more than they had in the Asheville hearing. Bartlett suggests that Champion's audacity, busing these workers in and "occupying" Knoxville, worked against the company. "They were, in the minds of many Tennesseans, intruders telling Tennessee to go to hell." The *Knoxville Journal* chimed in with its support the next morning. Its lead editorial read "Champion will have to close the mill." "A wave of anti-Champion hostility swept across East Tennessee," writes Bartlett.[42]

A compromise was finally proposed in mid-1988 when the North Carolina Division of Environmental Management approved a permit that allowed for eighty-five color-units in the Pigeon River at the North Carolina–Tennessee state line, slightly higher than the fifty color units the EPA permit had required. The final version, which came a year later, required Champion to meet the fifty-color-unit standard within three years. But by this time the fight over the Pigeon was no longer just about the color and smell of the water. Studies had shown high levels of dioxin, a known cancer-causing agent, in the water. Other studies suggested that communities along the Pigeon below Champion were suffering from higher than normal levels of certain types of cancer. The findings confirmed the suspicions of the workers on the ESOP Committee, who had seen their families and friends afflicted with what seemed like unusually high cancer rates.[43]

A class-action lawsuit filed by a group of Tennessee residents against Champion in 1991 charged the company with knowingly endangering residents' lives by discharging dioxin into the river. The suit was finally settled in 1994,[44] but it was not until December 1997, two months after Champion had announced that it was putting the Canton mill up for sale, that a permit was finally approved that all parties could agree to.[45] Higgins's claim at the time that the ESOP Committee was "opening up a dialog with environmental groups," and union local president Mike Coleman's promise to "run any mill we own with respect for people and the environment," must have sounded like pipe dreams to those familiar with this history.

Some of the most skeptical were the potential investment bankers that the ESOP Committee was courting to help fund the buyout. Adams described one of the committee's early strategizing sessions.

> We had to start thinking strategically. We had to analyze our political reality. Now the political reality was fairly clear. There were two major parts to it. One was that Champion's reputation was so widely known in banking circles that investors were staying away by the boatload. Their poor reputation for abuse of the environment and their reluctant efforts, belatedly, to do anything about, even the water, preceded everybody's potential bid. When investment bankers would come to town to talk to union members, the first question out of their mouths was "what is the situation with the environment?" They weren't talking about "can this mill make a profit? Can you change your work rules? Will you take a pay cut?" Didn't ask any of those questions. And before investment bankers ever started coming . . . we realized that [the environment] was one problem that was going to be facing the buyout. And it would face them first, because they could lose their jobs if they couldn't provide an answer to that.[46]

The ESOP Committee chose what seemed an unlikely answer in light of Champion's long history of battling environmentalists. The new potential owners would try cooperation instead of confrontation.

They would seek to establish a working relationship with local, regional, and national environmental organizations. The more the ESOP Committee considered the possibility the more it began to seem like one of those "just plain commonsense" proposals that were proving to be so effective. "We said, 'who do we need in this process?'" Higgins remembered. "Let's talk to environmentalist people, tell them our story, our side of the thing. And maybe they can help us with their input. . . . It's just pure old what makes sense. Break down the barriers of personalities or stigmas or whatever and let's start a dialog with those people it makes sense to have a dialog with. And we had nothing to lose, everything to gain. . . . Because environmental groups can relate to employees where they can't relate to big business."[47]

Sutton explained, "I think they were at a point that we both had a common enemy, Champion. We could both blame a lot of the past and a lot of the things on Champion. And, think about it, they had nothing to lose. Did they want to come out and set up a relationship with us just like they'd had with Champion? Or was there an opportunity here for all of us to sit down at the table and say how we as people, as stewards of our environment, as people concerned about our environment, go forward together. So it was a no-lose situation for them."[48] For Doug Gibson, "The river [was] the common ground. Because, I mean, it affects us. They don't want to see the plant shut down. But they want the river cleaned up, and we can understand where they're coming from on that."[49]

Still, an eighty-year adversarial relationship had left each side wary of the other. In a first tentative step to open the dialog, Adams and his wife, Margaret, accompanied Gregg and Higgins to Newport, Tennessee, to meet with representatives of the Dead Pigeon River group. Gregg's first impression was that the environmentalists "were no different than us." Gregg sensed that they were eager to talk. "They welcomed us with open arms," he said.[50] Indeed, some leaders in the environmental movement jumped at this new opportunity. Ginny Lindsey, co-director of the Clean Water Fund of North Carolina, wrote Higgins that her organization had always believed that "the region should have not only the good paying jobs that the mill has provided, but also a clean river." She expressed the organization's "support of a worker buyout of the Champion mill at Canton" and offered "to meet with you or other Union representatives to offer our support and to go over the recent agreement on Champion's permit."[51] In a similar vein, Charlotte Lackey of the Sierra Club wished the union "success in your effort" and urged the ESOP Committee to "please get in touch with me or any of our officers if we can help you in any way."[52] Such a drastic change in posture in the two months since Champion had put the mill up for sale was astounding. But this remarkable show of unity between paper mill workers and environmentalists came only after a series of meetings that, at least in the beginning, were rather tense.

Chris Just, the SACCO associate Adams had introduced to the ESOP Committee, played a key role in melting the icy relations between environmentalists and Champion workers. The ESOP Committee had been so impressed with the skills and knowledge that Just brought to the table that they asked him to serve with Adams as a paid consultant for the union. For his part, Just had become so committed to Local 507's cause that he left his job as director of Mountain Microenterprise to work full time for the union.

Just had friends in environmental organizations, and he arranged to take Sutton, Gregg, and Gibson to a number of their meetings. At one of these meetings, Gibson gave an eloquent account of the conflict workers felt at being economically dependent on an industry that was killing their rivers. At another, Sutton issued a heartfelt apology for his own role in damaging the environment and laid out a vision for a new kind of relationship with environmentalists where the new company would protect the environment and environmentalists would work to ensure economic stability.[53]

Just organized a meeting with leaders from environmental groups, and he found that they had been listening. Representatives from the Dogwood Alliance, the Sierra Club, the Clean Water Fund of North Carolina, Good Earth, and other organizations agreed to come to Local 507's union hall in Canton to begin discussions. Driving down Interstate 40 toward Canton, they must have noticed the caution sign reading, "BEWARE OF FOG FOR THE NEXT TEN MILES." The "fog" is actually the North Carolina Department of Transportation's delicate euphemism for the thick clouds that routinely drift over from the tall smokestacks reaching above the Canton paper mill. As they stood just off of Main Street in the Local 507 parking lot, taking in the busy little town with the smokestacks hovering like benevolent but quick-to-anger gods, they may have wondered just what they had gotten themselves into. Most had never been to Canton nor anywhere near a union hall. As Adams describes it, for most of them, the issue of Champion's environmental record had been "real but imaginary. It was a real issue; it's an issue today. But they had never met face to face with the people who had to carry out Champion's orders or lose their jobs."[54]

Committed as they were to cleaning up the environment, understanding as they did that people will resist anything that might endanger their livelihoods, they had never talked directly with the people who most understood the dangers of papermaking. To the environmentalists, for example, the chlorine bleaching process was a source of concern. It could, in theory, result in the release of poisonous materials into the water table and from there into the drinking water. To the workers, who wore gas masks on their belts and were trained to run if they saw a cloud of gas, the dangers were much more than theory; they were daily reality.

When the environmentalists filed into the large meeting room at Local 507, "you could have cut the air with a knife," remembered Higgins. "It was almost like negotiations. The union was sitting on one side and the environmental groups were sitting on the other. [It felt like] there was no real common ground."[55] There was tension and skepticism on both sides. "They were scared to death and we were scared to death," said Haney.[56] As Henson put it, "they couldn't believe that we were willing to sit down in the same room."[57] Kenny Sutton's frankness and sincerity began to melt the icy atmosphere in the room. "I always felt pretty comfortable," he said. "Because my beliefs are what they are, and I wasn't blowing smoke up their asses; I actually believed what I was telling them."[58]

Another factor that helped both sides lower their defenses was the union's insistence that the environmentalists sign a confidentiality agreement. Champion had been adamant that it would only accept a bid from the union if the ESOP Committee and anyone who worked for it would sign a strict confidentiality agreement. The company feared that if details of its financial situation and the proposed buy-out leaked out onto the shop floor and into the community, other potential bidders might back away. "This became a very serious problem in the long run, because the union leadership could not go out and talk about specifics," explained Adams. "They couldn't talk about the specific plan of the ESOP; they couldn't talk about the price that they knew they were bidding; they couldn't talk about the value of the asset that they were purchasing; they couldn't talk about how much people were going to have to invest on a monthly basis from their pay-checks. If they did, or if they even began to look like they were, or sound like they were talking about those details, Champion would jerk the chain of whichever banking house was involved."[59]

Later, when the ESOP Committee was trying to win the support of the union's rank and file, the strict confidentiality agreement would prove to be a liability. But the committee was able to turn it into an asset in this early meeting with environmentalists. "It gave the union members parity with the environmentalists," Adams said. The ESOP Committee "would learn something from the environmentalists about what specific concerns they had and they would know that the environmentalists couldn't go out and publish the fact in their own newsletters or newspapers."[60] The confidentiality agreement was a binding formality that made the union and the environmentalists equal partners with common interests. As soon as the agreement was signed, frank discussions began and new understandings began to develop; the environmentalists began to see that the union people who had ridden the buses to Asheville and Knoxville "were, in fact, being used by Champion." The two sides began to listen to each other and to find some common ground. As Gibson said, "The river is the common ground."[61]

In the ensuing discussions, the terms of the confidentiality agreement were violated only once, and this was not by grassroots environmentalists but by a University of North Carolina at Asheville professor. Dr. Richard Maas had developed a new method for removing toxic effluents from the water and had pitched it to the ESOP Committee as a potential solution to their problems. Whether Maas was so excited at the possibilities that he made careless and indiscreet comments or just did not take his agreement with the ESOP Committee members seriously because they lacked the formal education and economic power of others he had dealt with, Adams is certain that he almost killed the entire buyout effort at this early stage. Two years later, the memory of the episode still evoked anger in Adams:

> Maas voiced it around with his staff that he had met with the union. One of his staff members happened to be a neighbor and called me up and told me all about the meeting [between the ESOP Committee and environmentalists]. And I said to him, "you know, your boss has breeched confidentiality. And that is a potential for a lawsuit. If Champion hears that you've been over there talking with the union and that they've been talking with you about what they're trying to do and what they know . . . Champion has a confidentiality agreement that says [the union] couldn't bid, and that means 2,200 jobs gone. So your boss, your academic leader, needs to know what he's done." And this guy told me, "if you go talk with him I'll lose my job." I said, "your job or 2,200 jobs. But the principle is he signed a paper saying he would not talk about this to anybody, and so did his colleague. And he has talked about it with you and I don't know who else."[62]

Adams immediately made an appointment with Maas, which Maas subsequently canceled "because he had to go to South America and advise some families that were organizing shrimp farms on the Pacific coast," said Adams.

> When he got back, all he wanted to do was talk with me about that. I said, "Richard, I'm not here to talk about your adventures working for the capitalists down in South America who are building shrimp farms. I'm here to talk with you about a contract of confidentiality that you signed in the union hall. And I want you to know that your colleague, Phil Neal, was talking with a personal friend of mine in the checkout line at the French Broad Co-op, saying that if the workers buy this out we're going to get a contract to do X." And I said, "two weeks ago, on a Saturday morning, as I was washing the breakfast dishes, I got a telephone call from another of your colleagues telling me how delighted he was, and how much he was looking forward to working with the men at Champion, because our buyout plans were working so well." I said, "so you've breeched the confidentiality of those men,

and you have potentially put their jobs at risk." And I said, "I don't know whether they'll sue or not, but I can tell you I will." And he hasn't spoken to me since. And he's now the Chairman of the Air Quality Board for Buncombe County.[63]

The incident prompted a letter from Neal to Higgins concerning a follow-up meeting scheduled for January 7, in which Neal gave assurance that "[Dr. Maas and I] recognize that this visit and the conversations taking place then should be confidential, both in your interest and ours," but discussions with Maas and his methods of purifying water proceeded no further.[64]

The Canton and subsequent meetings with environmentalists won the public endorsement and support by major environmental organizations of the union's efforts at a very critical time. North Carolina's state politicians, heretofore reluctant to side with environmentalists because they didn't want to be perceived as doing anything that would lead to loss of jobs and reluctant to criticize environmentalists too stridently because they represented a well-organized and well-funded lobby, now had a new line. They could support the union's efforts to purchase the mill, praising it as a way to save 2,200 jobs, and keep the economy of western North Carolina healthy. At the same time, they could brag that they were siding with the Sierra Club and the North Carolina Clean Water Fund in efforts to find a creative solution to the long-running conflicts around the Canton mill. These two environmental organizations, "stayed the course," according to Adams. "They wrote letters to the editor; they never revealed that they had meetings with the union; they met with other environmental groups and held them at bay, said, 'let's wait and see what happens.'"[65]

The ESOP Committee immediately made several moves that demonstrated its good faith. The union men hired John Runkle, a prominent environmental lawyer from Chapel Hill, who consulted with the environmentalists throughout the process. They began contacting research organizations, such as the Chlorine Free Products Association, about more environmentally friendly ways to produce paper. They requested information on color removal from the American Canoe Association, once a bitter foe of Champion. And they began identifying possible environmental consulting organizations they could contract with should the buyout go through.

Champion officials, in their Connecticut corporate offices, must have been puzzled when they started reading letters to the editor from organizations they had fought tooth and nail supporting the potential new mill owners. These workers were building coalitions between groups that they had expended enormous energy to weaken by keeping them divided. In just two months, the union had mustered more political savvy and carried out a more effective campaign than any of Champion's highly paid executive officers or consulting firms had ever been able to conceive. The "active support [of environmentalists], I think, astonished Champion," said Adams. "I don't think Champion understands, to this day, that those secret meetings that we had were a political key."[66] "Just plain old what makes sense," as Higgins described it.[67] The river had indeed proven to be the common ground.

CHAPTER 6

Building a Groundswell of Support

The strategic alliance between Champion workers and environmental activists gave the buyout effort a tremendous boost. It improved relations with elected officials, state and regional union leaders, business organizations, churches, schools, and the local community—all of the groups the ESOP Committee had targeted. It was now possible to support the big paper mill in Canton and sound environmental management at the same time. After more than eighty years of confrontations, workers and environmentalists were now allies against the common enemy, Champion.

The *Asheville Citizen-Times,* whose editorial page had tiptoed through this minefield for years trying to appease both environmentalists and Champion without alienating either, seized the opportunity. Arguing that local control of the mill would be best for everyone concerned, the paper asked, "Who would you trust as an environmental steward: a corporation with headquarters in another state or even another country, or an outfit that's locally controlled?" It quoted Higgins's promises for an economically and environmentally sound business. His words, it said, "represent no change from the feelings of many Champion workers of a bygone era." For the first time, the paper acknowledged an important distinction. The workers were not company pawns passively accepting Champion's claims that it was doing all it could to protect the environment. "Over the years," the *Citizen-Times* concluded, "many Champion workers have reflected the concerns of others in the area by saying they, too, were not happy with a dirty river and polluted air. Many a conversation began with 'If it were up to me. . . .' With luck, it will be up to them."[1] The *Citizen-Times* no longer looked to corporate headquarters in Connecticut for the voice of Champion; now it turned to Local 507's union hall in Canton.

This remarkable shift, which began with overtures from the ESOP Committee, gelled at a meeting held at the union hall in early January 1998. After that meeting, the Dogwood Alliance, Sierra Club,

Appalachian Voices, the North Carolina Clean Water Fund, and the Earth Island Institute were all either voicing public support for the buyout effort or were at least withholding public criticism. But while the ESOP Committee had scored a huge political victory in winning the support of the environmental community, it faced some uncertainties with its own rank and file.

Local 507's executive committee learned that one union member intended to put a motion on the floor at the next general membership meeting to rescind the earlier motion committing union funds to the buyout effort. As it turned out, the motion failed by a vote of 4 to 70, but the fact that it had been introduced at all concerned some members of the committee.[2] It served as a reminder that support from the rank and file always came with a measure of skepticism. "I wouldn't say everyone was wholehearted for the idea," was the way Gregg put it. "There was maybe a few little areas that had a lot of skepticism. 'How can you guys?' 'What can you do?' 'There's going to be another paper mill come in or Champion's going to find a buyer and just go ahead and shut down.'"[3]

The skepticism on the part of both employees and managers was quite understandable. Most still believed that Champion would never consider selling the mills to union-led employees. The ESOP Committee now knew that this was not true, that Champion was close to accepting the union as a qualified bidder and that the union was already involved in serious negotiations with a potential funder. But the strict confidentiality agreement between Local 507 and Champion made it impossible to share these details. So while they now knew that they could own the mills, and that they were capable of functioning as owners, they could not share the evidence with the rank and file.

Just days after Local 507 announced that Champion had accepted it as a qualified bidder, it swore in James Hutchinson as its new president. While Hutch had a reputation as a fair-minded man who was not afraid to stand up for workers, he had limited experience as a union officer. Adams had said early and repeatedly that the effort would need the full support of the local and international union to succeed. Even with as much potential as Hutch had shown for becoming a strong union leader, this was not the best time to be learning the ropes.

As yet, the buyout effort did not have a financial backer. The top candidate was ACS, which had already funded more than forty employee buyouts. The day after Hutch was sworn in as Local 507's president, representatives of ACS sat down in the union hall with L. J. Rose, Bob Smith, and the ESOP Committee to discuss a possible partnership. Smith and the ACS representatives left Canton after five days, leaving Rose to deliberate with the ESOP Committee over whether or not to partner with ACS. In between meetings, Rose was on the phone with Smith, keeping him appraised of progress and his own concerns with ACS.[4]

In spite of Rose's misgivings, by the eighteenth of January the parties had reached a tentative agreement. ACS would be the union's major financial backer for the buyout and would submit a competitive bid to Champion as soon as the details could be worked out. Higgins expressed his enthusiasm in an *Asheville Citizen-Times* account of the deal, which claimed that no other potential buyers had come forward.[5] The article did mention one possibility that must have sent a jolt of fear through the Canton plant. It claimed that a major player in the paper industry with a reputation for successfully fighting unionization might be interested in purchasing the Canton system. To many union workers in the paper industry this particular corporation was no less than the devil incarnate. "We as a union hated them," explained Haney, "because they have damned unions, they have really treated their people bad as far as being union active. They're just one of the worst. I mean they try every way in the world to beat out unions."[6]

Muzzled by the confidentiality agreement, the ESOP Committee had become extremely sensitive to public opinion. It now saw its efforts to educate and build a coalition as critical to the success of the buyout. Besides the relationship it had forged with the environmental community, it had won the active support of the international, which designed an educational brochure titled *Common Folks with Common Sense and a Common Cause!* The brochure gave a brief account of Champion's plans and portrayed Local 507 members as working-class heroes who had embarked on a "bold and daring move of their own" and who needed and deserved support. The title reflected the ESOP Committee's fundamental strategy. Their strength, they were discovering, lay in the very fact that they simply were what they were, hard-working citizens committed to saving the economic base of their community. They had no glitzy presentational skills, only integrity and a willingness to do whatever it would take. They were more comfortable with and more trusting of a handshake and a verbal promise than a team of high-priced corporate lawyers who knew all the angles. Their straightforward, honest approach stood out in the world of high finance in which deception and stealth were the norm.

While the financial support of the local was adequate for the time being, it was clear that the union treasury alone would not be enough. The initial payments to SACCO and ACS came from money that had been set aside for operating funds during contract negotiations. Since the current contract was scheduled to expire before the year was out, the treasury needed to be replenished.[7] ACS required a monthly retainer of $20,000, and up to $5,000 per month expenses. The process of evaluating the assets for sale and the viability of purchasing the mills, along with preparing a bid to submit was expected to take at least six months. In addition, the union was paying SACCO $2,500 per month.[8] Local 507 was on track either to face negotiations with Champion or set up a new company with empty pockets.

As part of their work as paid consultants, Adams and Just began exploring ways that the union might raise additional funds. Drawing on his fund-raising experience and contacts, Just began contacting organizations in search of grant money. He became frustrated when one potential funder after another asked what resources the ESOP Committee already had. He later described it as feeling like a recent college graduate seeking his first job. "Every employer expects you to have experience and no one will give you the first job so you can get experience."[9]

Two organizations, the North Carolina Rural Economic Development Center and Advantage West, showed some interest. While pursuing these possibilities, Just began looking for ways that he could demonstrate to potential funders that there was already strong financial support. Soon after he had approached Advantage West with a request for $100,000, the organization conducted a study of how the local economy would be affected if Champion left. It clearly documented that the results would be disastrous, and Just hit on the idea of taking the study before the Haywood County Board of Supervisors, with a request for funding to support the buyout campaign. The idea would later prove to be a key political move.[10]

While Just worked at raising funds to cover the ESOP Committee's operating costs, ACS gathered a group of investment bankers at the Canton YMCA, hoping to entice them into investing in the buyout.[11] As the prospective investors strolled through the plant they got a quick introduction to the dangers that the would-be worker-owners lived with daily. Workers sharing coffee and swapping stories in Local 507's union hall still chuckle over the shocked expressions of the nattily dressed bankers, just off the plane from New York City, when they were handed gas mask bags and told to "run like hell" if they saw a cloud, which would be toxic chlorine gas.[12]

L. J. Rose still had reservations about working with ACS. During these early negotiations with the investment firm, he stayed in constant touch with Bob Smith, the union's regional vice-president. After a long career of negotiating union business with corporate representatives who kept their cards close to their chest and answered pointed questions with vague generalities, Rose couldn't shake a general uneasiness about ACS. During this period, he was frequently heard to mention that he had some concerns with ACS. Rose feared that the union might be trading a long-standing, though imperfect, traditional company/union relationship for a new company/union relationship in which the ground rules were uncertain. What would the union's role be in this new relationship? What legal recourse would the union have if the primary funder began violating workplace rights? It was all new ground for a seasoned union official with a healthy measure of skepticism.[13]

With the encouragement of Adams and Just, the ESOP Committee, riding the success of its commonsense approach to the environmental community, continued to seek support from other constituencies. Just had been hoping for open support from governmental bodies, which he was sure would help his fundraising efforts.[14] Adams and the committee saw other advantages to support from local and state governments. Public comments from governmental officials would bring free publicity. It would encourage other influential people who had been silent on the buyout to speak out. Potential funders might be more willing to take risks on the venture knowing that local governments were supporting it. And Champion's home office might be pushed to give up some of the tight control it had been exerting over the process. But the downside of the plain old commonsense approach was a lack of experience. While the strategy was clearly a good one, the committee did not know how to begin. Higgins explained: "We were trying to contact each of the political officials, from Haywood County, from Canton, from Waynesville. We tried to get the governor, and we couldn't get to the governor because we didn't know how to do this, because none of us had ever done anything like this."[15]

While he was always reluctant to take a public leadership role, Adams stood ready to use his skills and contacts to ease the process along when necessary. "Frank helped us in the process and gave us a general outline of who and how we needed to conduct a community campaign and a political campaign," continued Higgins. "But we had to do the calls and the legwork and so forth ourselves."[16] Adams would call it "education," the kind of education he had devoted his life to. Put the knowledge, skills, and contacts into the hands of those who have the most at stake and trust that they will discover an effective way to reach the goal. What's more, they will grow in the process.

Higgins described one of the political lessons that the committee learned: "[We] did find out that in political support you have to build a groundswell in the community first and [with] the area politicians. And then go up to the next level, to your local representatives in the state legislature. And then they, along with support from the North Carolina AFL-CIO, and every group that we could think of to contact, they would put pressure on the governor's office to get involved."[17] It would be a grand irony for Jim Hunt, a Democratic governor of North Carolina, to come out in support of Smoky Mountain Local 507. Only forty years earlier another man who would be elected as a Democratic governor of the state had stood in the Canton mill before a coffin and preached a derisive "Death to the Union" funeral oration. It would be a testament to the political knowledge and wisdom that the ESOP Committee had developed, an affirmation of the theory of education that Adams held so deeply.

The Committee soon discovered that one of its biggest barriers to building local support was Champion itself. The Committee was hamstrung by the company's insistence that no details of its operations or plans concerning the sale of the Haywood County mills be released to the public. According to Higgins, Champion let them know, in no uncertain terms, that "if there's any real details of the bidding process [released], then you're out." In fact, the company threatened as much after the union's public announcement that its letter of intent to purchase had been accepted. "Champion striped our legs over the letter of intent in the newspaper. They said, 'you've broken our confidentiality agreement.'"[18]

By mid-February the committee faced another dilemma. The local's money was running out. "We were having to pay ACS by the month," said Higgins. "And the treasury of the union wasn't that big. And we had to pay our wages and our expenses and so forth while we were out of work." As Just had already experienced firsthand, to raise money the committee would need community support. And yet, doing so might prompt Champion to declare a breach of the confidentiality agreement and push them out of the process. "We kind of had to take a chance with Champion. We said, 'well, we've got our legs striped. We have to gamble whether or not they'll kick us out or whether they won't, but we have to do it.'"[19]

The ESOP Committee decided to broaden its campaign but at the same time run it as a stealth campaign. "[We contacted] area churches, area businesses, area civic groups, and we did that somewhat on the sly as best we could, until we got what we thought was a network, a big enough network of support that made sense to announce to the general public," said Higgins.[20] While the committee was building its network, Champion reacted to an *Asheville Citizen-Times* editorial that criticized the company's environmental record and came out in support of the union's efforts. While Champion's claim that the article constituted a violation of the confidentiality agreement was a stretch, the ESOP Committee thought it prudent to avoid antagonizing the company. Chris Just met with two local journalists who had been covering the story, Peggy Gosselin, Canton bureau chief of the *Enterprise Mountaineer* in Waynesville, and Tim Reid, business editor of the *Asheville Citizen-Times*, and asked them to be careful of divulging too many specifics. "They were wonderful and supportive," Just said. "They went by the rules that we asked for the rest of the way."[21] Adams added that Gosselin provided the "fullest, most accurate coverage of any journalist" who covered the buyout.[22]

On February 19, the ESOP Committee finally got an audience with Jerry Sutton, the director of Governor Hunt's western office. Higgins, as the ESOP Committee's chair, opened the presentation. The committee had prepared carefully; Higgins gave a history of their work and an account of where it stood at present. He went into a fair amount of detail on the financial aspects, passing around handouts with estimates of how much money had already been spent and how much would likely be needed. Jerry Sutton handed out some political advice that the ESOP Committee had already discovered on its own: start locally and build support up to the higher levels of government. Regarding fund-raising, Hunt's representative echoed the earlier words of Just. It would be easier for the governor's office to lend support if the local county commissioners gave vocal and financial support. "They should be in Raleigh knocking on doors for you," he said. "They have the power to do something." Another of the governor's representatives suggested that the union should seek support from surrounding counties.[23]

Higgins responded that a meeting between the ESOP Committee and officials from surrounding counties had already been set up and that he would get to work on setting up a meeting with Haywood officials. But for the most part, the meeting with the governor's representatives yielded little practical assistance. The ESOP Committee had been acting for several weeks on the observation that "the more people you have talking for you the better chance you will have of getting the money."[24]

Even before the meeting with Governor Hunt's representatives, the ESOP Committee had sought the support of Robert Carpenter, state senator for Haywood and Buncombe counties. Four days after they contacted Carpenter, he met with Hunt. Carpenter called the union hall early the following morning before the ESOP Committee met to report that Hunt had been interested in the committee's progress but had made no commitments at all. Hunt, an experienced lawyer who was serving an unprecedented fourth term as governor, was carefully walking a legal and political tightrope. He would later explain that open support of one bidder over another by a government official could be seen as a violation of the law. A more compelling reason may have been North Carolina's history as a staunchly antiunion state, and support of any union initiative could have hurt him politically. Carpenter did say that he was trying to arrange a credit line for the union with First Union National Bank, an institution for which he had once been a vice-president.[25]

While the committee was making great strides in its campaign to build community support, its struggle for support from its own workforce was floundering. As Kenny Sutton put it, "there was times there that we had more community support than we had support inside the facility. A lot of times."[26] The rank and file were growing suspicious of the vague generalities they were hearing. Here's how Higgins described it: "You've got thirteen hundred employees and someone would say, "How's it going? Can you tell us something? Who's bidding? How much are we going to bid? What are the details of the bid?" You couldn't divulge anything except to say, 'We're working on it. We'll give you the details when we can. At this time we can't communicate anything with you.'" The confidentiality agreement, which kept the committee from being open and forthcoming, strained them, inside and outside the plant. Higgins explained that, "for that matter, we couldn't discuss any details with even our wives. If word leaked out of any of the real details of the deal into the news media or had spread in any form or fashion we could be kicked out of the bidding process."[27] Some accused the committee of having something to hide and charged that they were only benefiting themselves, according to Gibson. "It feels like they put a noose around your neck and they're just slowly tightening it up. I mean it was basically just within these four walls, the stuff that we went through."[28]

While pressures from without drove the committee members closer together, the mounting tensions and overwhelming weight of the task they had taken on led to some angry confrontations in committee meetings. Just described a near "brutal fight" between Higgins and Henson. Higgins, according to Just, felt that Henson was being too resistant and unwilling to take chances and was slowing the process. "They were quickly up on their feet, nose to nose, about to come to blows," according to Just.[29] As would happen many times in the ensuing months, when things began to fall apart, one of the committee members would step up to the plate and get the process back on track. It was part of a team chemistry that was developing. They were learning to play off of each other's strengths and weaknesses and could readily pinch hit for one another when necessary. This time it was Sutton who intervened with the calm hand, breaking up the fight and suggesting that it was time for a break.

"Henson had turned white," said Just, "but he wasn't as white as I was." Just was so shaken that, although he had quit smoking years before, he bummed a cigarette and lit it with trembling hands. Not quite sure how he should proceed as a paid consultant, he called Adams, who told him that he would have to get Higgins and Henson talking again, settle it, and move ahead. There was just too much at stake to let this stop them for long. Before the committee reconvened, Just shared this with Higgins, who had already come to the same conclusion on his own. Higgins reconvened the committee "with a sincere and humble apology for his behavior," according to Just. Henson responded with his own apology.[30]

After discussing Senator Carpenter's account of his meeting with Hunt, the committee heard from David Jenkins of the American Canoe Association, who presented some research indicating that there would be a market for chlorine-free paper. According to Jenkins, although the cost would be high, the new customer base would make it worthwhile.[31] After listening politely to Jenkins and asking a few technical questions, the committee turned to preparing for that evening's informational meeting, which was open to all salaried and hourly employees. With pressures from environmentalists to invest in technology for a mill they didn't even own yet, pressures from fellow workers to give a full account of the progress, legal threats from Champion not to do so, and tensions within their group mounting, the committee handled the evening informational session with remarkable professionalism and grace. "The meeting went pretty well," noted L. J. Rose, "except for one salaried employee who made an ass of himself."[32]

On the following afternoon, the Haywood County Commissioners came to Local 507's union hall to get an update on the progress of the buyout attempt. As Governor Hunt's representatives had recommended, Higgins also informed the commissioners "how [they] might possibly help this process along."[33] Within the week, Higgins would formalize this with requests for $100,000 from Haywood County and $50,000 from Buncombe County.[34]

The ESOP Committee would win some desperately needed support if the requests were granted. Obviously, the money would help replenish the union's dwindling bank account, and the public support would help them attract other funders and increase the pressure on the state government to take a more active role. Executives at Champion's home office in Connecticut may have cast an eye toward the little town that Peter Thompson and Reuben Robertson had bankrolled and that generations of Champion workers had built and realized that they might face a serious public relations problem if they turned their back on it now.

Higgins and Sutton appeared before the Buncombe county commissioners to make their case for financial assistance. When the commissioners made no decision, the entire ESOP Committee appeared at the next meeting to answer questions.[35] Eventually, both the Buncombe and Haywood county commissioners were convinced that the buyout effort represented the best chance to save the local economy. They voted to grant the $50,000 and $100,000, respectively, that the committee had requested.[36]

But Haywood County's financial contribution was not without controversy. In the eighty plus years that Champion had operated in the county, its workers had enjoyed certain privileges. With an average salary that was roughly twice that of other local workers, jobs at Champion were coveted. Haywood workers who were not part of the Champion family were sometimes "jealous because you're making this kind of wages." According to Sutton, the jealousies sometimes led to a kind of elitism.

> Maybe my son tried to [get hired at the plant] and he couldn't get on. Then you had people inside Champion that worked for Champion for years that may have thought they were a little bit

better than John over there that worked at Dayco [another plant in Haywood County] or worked at the filling station or what not. And acted like they were better. So maybe not all of the perception was bad from folks on the outside. I mean we, as hard as it is to say, I think we hold some responsibility for that. Maybe we thought we were a little bit above some folks because we're now making 40 grand a year and you look around and everybody's making 20. And maybe we showed that off a little more than we should've. And maybe we weren't as humble as we ought to be.[37]

When Haywood's county commissioners voted to approve the ESOP Committee's request for $100,000, some of this simmering jealousy rose to the surface. In a letter to the *Enterprise Mountaineer,* J. A. Cochran called it "absolutely disgusting to see the local elected officials jump on the Champion bandwagon again by giving $100,000 of taxpayer money to the union. Remembering that "Dayco also had several hundred high-paying jobs, . . . a large annual payroll and considerable tax revenue to contribute," Cochran wondered where the commissioners had been when this producer of rubber hoses and automotive belts had closed. "It seems they [Champion] are the only ones in Haywood County that matter," he wrote, "and everyone else is second-rate."[38]

But in the end, the memory of Dayco's departure and the effect it had on the county's economy worked to Local 507's advantage. "We had those other people saying, 'Look, we can't afford to lose those jobs, so help them.' And that made things better," Haney explained.[39] "One of the guys that was a county commissioner actually worked at Dayco," Sutton remembered. "And he says, 'I know it can go down. We said they'd never close and I seen them shut the doors on us.'"[40] When Higgins explained "the importance that [Champion's payroll] had on the economic multiplier in Haywood County," the commissioners decided that investing $100,000 in the union's effort was a small gamble against the risk of losing a payroll nearly twice the size it had lost with Dayco's closure.[41]

Neighboring Buncombe County's gift of $50,000 drew strong local support. The *Asheville Citizen-Times* called it "the right thing" and said that it made "obvious sense," citing figures such as the "$12 million of the company's $15 million medical insurance plan [that] was spent in Buncombe County" and the fact that "Champion employees pump an estimated $20 million into Buncombe through retail sales." As County Manager Wanda Green summed it up, "There's not much magic about that county line when it comes to the impact the loss of Champion would have on all of us."[42]

Meanwhile, Rose was not alone in his concerns about ACS. On Friday of the same week in which Higgins and the committee were updating the commissioners, Sutton phoned Adams. He reported that the committee's effort to garner community support was going very well. But, beyond that, Sutton was concerned that ACS was operating too much in the dark, making decisions that directly affected the committee without consulting them first. After hearing Sutton out, Adams faxed a response the same afternoon. It was one of the rare occasions in which Adams offered advice, but even with his advice he prodded Sutton to take action for himself. Adams was certain that ACS, as a partner, would act in the best interests of Local 507. But Adams was sensitive to the committee's fears that they would be shut out of the process, leaving them with an investment boss to replace the corporate boss and little chance for greater democracy on the shop floor. He advised Sutton that "Local 507 must let your partner know what your bottom line expectations [are] as the next stage in the buy-out unfolds." He urged the committee to seek "written clarity" on the exact time when ACS would submit the bid. If the sale went through and became public before there was a financial commitment from the Buncombe and Haywood county commissioners, these potential sources of funding and support could dry up fast. He also advised Sutton that the union should insist on seeing the bid and having details of the contract explained before the bid would be submitted. He urged the ESOP Committee to develop "a business plan, a market plan, and the financial plan, including exit strategies and costs," as soon as possible. Finally, Adams urged the committee to hire local legal counsel and to have them present when they met with ACS. "This is a short-term cost," he said, "but one which will bear long term investment returns."[43]

At a strategy session in early March of 1998, the ESOP Committee decided to build on its success with the Haywood and Buncombe county commissioners and to intensify its campaign for community and government support. Just had a friend in the state government, Rick Carlisle, who had recently been named acting director of commerce by Governor Hunt. He called Carlisle, who suggested that the union send someone to Raleigh to meet with him and other Hunt administration officials. According to Just, Adams told him that they should remain in the background, helping Sutton and Higgins with research when necessary, but being very careful to let the ESOP Committee speak for itself.[44]

Dale Carroll, executive director of Advantage West, took a different approach, according to Just. Advantage West was a partner of the North Carolina Rural Economic Development Center, whose purpose was to open up new investment opportunities in rural areas of the state. The organization had been cool to the ESOP Committee's request for funding until Carroll learned of the upcoming trip to Raleigh and the possibility of a meeting with a representative of the governor's office. Now he arranged for the flight himself through his connections in the state Department of Commerce and insisted on going along as part of the entourage.[45] In the end, the Rural Economic Development Center and Advantage West each contributed $25,000 to the buyout effort.

While nothing concrete came of the first trip to Raleigh, Higgins and Sutton did make one contact who would later prove to be extremely helpful. Joan Weld, one of Governor Hunt's top assistants, was about to retire from a long career in public service. When Higgins and Sutton sat down with her, they "were naive enough, but yet thorough enough to be able to not be afraid of the political system, the political machine, if you will," explained Higgins. "We told Joan Weld, 'we're just factory workers. We're just trying to protect our jobs, keep our jobs. Here's the economic impact. Here's the things that we found out during this whole due diligence process. This is what it means to 2,200 families. We need your help.'"[46] Weld would promise nothing except to study the committee's request for assistance, and Higgins and Sutton returned to Canton largely unaware of the deep impression they had made on Weld, who would later become one of their strongest and most influential allies in state government.

Thirty-five miles northeast of Canton, in the small college town of Mars Hill, North Carolina, Dan Ray, the son of a lifelong Champion employee, had been following news of the buyout effort in the press. In the early 1970s, Ray had left his hometown of Iron Duff, which lies just ten miles up Interstate 40 from Canton, to enroll as an undergraduate at Mars Hill College. While there he became active in the college's Community Development Institute and went on to build an impressive career as an expert in nonprofit organizational structure. In 1997 he had returned to western North Carolina to help establish the Institute at Mars Hill College, which worked to place students in community-based service learning projects through which they could practice their research skills while contributing to community development.[47]

In a sense Ray represented the very thing that Local 507's members had fought hard for, had won, and were now fighting to save: a high enough standard of living with economic security that their sons and daughters would have options. As Doug Gibson put it: "By having my job secure it means that if my son or daughter decide they want to go to school I have the opportunity to furnish them with the opportunity. That would make it easier on them. In turn, if they come back to the community, that's going to help the whole community."[48] So when Ray contacted the ESOP Committee requesting a meeting, Gibson and the other ESOP Committee members saw one of these sons that they had provided with an opportunity of returning home to help the community.

In the beginning, Ray seemed to be a natural fit. He listened to the accounts of the union's success, the support it had received from the international, the environmental community, local and state government, and he proposed using marketing and public relations techniques to expand this effort. In a stroke of irony, he recommended that the union hire Price McNabb, the same public relations firm that Champion had hired in the 1980s to clean up its public image as it battled environmentalists. Ray pushed the ESOP Committee to step out a little and take some more risks. He encouraged the union to begin operating as if it already were a corporation, to come up with a name, and to name a chief executive officer for the new company.[49]

The campaign, which would be dubbed "Back the Buyout," would be organized around four themes. The first theme would capitalize

on Champion's tradition and its long history in the area. It would highlight the fact that the current workforce represented families who had
been manufacturing paper in Haywood County for nearly one hundred
years. It would remind people of a simpler time, when managers were
neighbors and workers felt like every hour they worked benefited their
town and neighborhoods. To reflect this theme of tradition, the new
company would be called Sunburst Papers, a name with deep historical roots in the area.[50] Legend had it that in the earliest days, when
Reuben Robertson and Peter Thompson were searching for timber to
harvest for pulp, Robertson stood at the headwaters of the Pigeon River,
awed by the beauty of the sun rising over the mountains, and decided
to name the sawmill town Sunburst. Though the town no longer
existed, its memory was strong among local residents, and people still
called the area around nearby Lake Logan "Sunburst." As Ray would
later say, "The name Sunburst was the employees' way of getting back
to their origins."[51] Back the Buyout would also seek to shift responsibility onto Champion, implying that it owed the community one more
investment, selling the mills to its employees.[52]

Back the Buyout's second theme would emphasize the economic
angle. If Champion were to shut down or slash its workforce, the
results would be disastrous for the entire region. But the union was
offering a chance to turn impending disaster into a win-win situation
by protecting the economic base of the entire region, protecting jobs,
offering the opportunity for greater control of the community's own
wealth-generating capacity, and creating a local corporate headquarters instead of the current one, isolated far away in Connecticut.[53]

Next, the campaign would tout the advantages of employee stock
ownership. The employees would naturally be more invested in a long-
term sustainable operation, since, after all, they were the ones who
would have to live with the results. The ESOP structure would make
better use of employee knowledge, since the ones with the most intimate knowledge of the papermaking process would now be directly
involved in making production decisions. And for these same reasons,
the employees would be more likely than anyone else to take steps to
protect the environment.[54]

The final theme of Back the Buyout would highlight the community's interconnectedness. Since nearly everyone in Canton and

Wayresville either worked for Champion or had a relative who did, the entire community, not just the workers, should be made to feel like part owners of Sunburst Papers. Those who were claiming that Champion workers were pampered and consistently granted special favors needed to see a larger perspective. This was the community's mill, and its success would be the community's success. As evidence of this, the buyout and subsequent stock offerings would include all employees who wished to participate, not just union members.[55]

Lenny Sutton saw Ray as a potential asset. "Dan was very good at communication. And he knew a lot of people that could get us to people that we needed to know." Still, he had reservations about Ray's style and his loyalty to the community he came from. "He was flamboyant. He wouldn't be a buddy of mine. I think he forgot where he was raised."[56] When Price McNabb suggested to Ray that the ESOP Committee should attempt to "deunionize" the campaign, Sutton enthusiastically agreed.[57] Adams had insisted on working through the union, but Ray and Sutton believed that this would be a liability for the Back the Buyout campaign. "At Frank's insistence, we touted it as a 'union buyout,'" Sutton said. "We learned pretty early on that that wasn't getting us anywhere. It wasn't getting us a lot of support that we felt like we needed out there, because people were afraid to tie themselves to a 'union buyout.' And I think that was one of the early mistakes that Frank led us down the road on. But probably if we would have been a little bit more politically savvy and understood what we were going through we wouldn't have made that mistake. We'd of touted it from the very beginning as an 'employee buyout, led by the union.'"[58]

With Sutton operating as the point man in strategizing with the Mars Hill Institute and Price McNabb, a subtle shift occurred in the decision-making process. Up to this point, largely due to the influence of Adams and SACCO, all strategic decisions and public statements had been made by the ESOP Committee. Adams and Just, with the support of Rose, had given all information directly to the committee and had helped them to see all of their options, but they had scrupulously stepped back and allowed the committee to work on its own. The Institute at Mars Hill and Price McNabb brought more of a traditional "paid professional" approach to the table. Price McNabb sent the institute a "Timeline/To Do List," which planned out the details of the campaign for the entire month of March. The plan included little input from the committee, and Sutton was only contacted to inform him of what his role was to be at any given time.[59]

The Price McNabb/Institute plan called for a series of community awareness meetings culminating in a major news conference in Haywood County that would "have a pep rally feel." Employee representatives would meet with newspaper editorial boards to win their support. Even public school children would have a role. They would organize a letter-writing campaign to urge Champion officials to "help our parents save their jobs!" At the press conference, which would be timed to occur while the union's bid was on the table, the new company's name would be revealed and the new CEO would be introduced.[60]

On the surface, all of these moves were advancing the buyout effort, but underneath they were sowing seeds of dissension. While in the beginning Ray had been willing to listen to the committee members, treating them as equal partners, Just noticed that as the campaign heated up, "Dan's approach changed to directive, ordering, taking charge. For example, he made a verbal agreement that the Institute would work on a contingency basis, taking a percentage of the money that the Institute helped raise." For the ESOP Committee, such a verbal commitment was ironclad. Later, Ray handed Just a contract to take to the committee that called for a $5,000 payment upfront. The ESOP Committee rejected the contract outright, and communications between the committee and the institute became strained.[61]

On March 18, ACS sent to Champion's headquarters its letter of intent to purchase the Canton and Waynesville mills and associated Dairy Pak plants. The mailing included a cover letter addressed to Champion's chairman and CEO Richard Olson, quoting the bid for the entire Canton system at $186.6 million. It included a letter of financial support from the senior vice-president of ABN-AMRO Bank and another from Enron Capital & Trade executive Mark Lay, son of the soon-to-be infamous Enron CEO Kenneth Lay. Finally, the bid package contained a letter signed by all six members of the ESOP Committee that included detailed figures on employee compensation and stated the union's willingness to negotiate a new contract that represented a 15 percent reduction in compensation.[62]

With the bid in, the ESOP Committee turned its full attention to the community campaign. Sutton made a presentation before an interdenominational gathering of local ministers and other church leaders, who voted to endorse and publicly support the buyout bid.[63] Local 507, with its first president and its current president both Baptist ministers, had always had close ties to the faith community, and it was now clear that this relationship remained solid.

The press conference that Price McNabb and the Institute at Mars Hill had recommended took place on Thursday, March 26. Presiding were Canton's mayor, C. W. Hardin, and Clayton Davis of the North Carolina Department of Agriculture, who had been named co-chairs of the Back the Buyout committee. Hardin announced the selection of the name "Sunburst" and launched into a description of the history of the name and the paper mill's deep ties to the area. Davis stuck close to the script outlined by Price McNabb, arguing that the mills' closing would represent a $200 million impact on the regional economy. Sunburst Papers heralded "a new day with new promise," Davis said. And for those who had complained that Champion workers were simply being coddled as they always had, he called the buyout "a community project, not a political project." Higgins took the stage and announced that Terry Brubaker, an executive with a long and impressive background in the paper industry, had been named the president and CEO of the new employee-owned company.[64]

Almost as soon as the bid was in, communications between ACS and the ESOP Committee began to break down. Many close to the buyout felt that the bid did not reflect what ACS had agreed to, either contractually or in spirit. The rift highlighted the growing political awareness among the ESOP Committee, who now critically examined every transaction carried out in their name.

CHAPTER 7

A Battle for the New Company's Soul

Even as the bid was on the table, other interested parties began to come forward. At one committee meeting, Rose disclosed that a Champion official had told him that the Swedish company Enso had approached Champion about partnering with the Ukrainian paper company ELO and submitting a bid for the Canton and Waynesville plants. According to Rose, who was alarmed at the possibility of competing against a team of these two international corporations, another major player in the industry was now in the picture. This company, which had a widespread reputation for busting unions, contacted Brubaker, Sunburst's new CEO, and offered to contribute and thereby help raise the union's bid. The possibility of being partners with a union buster rankled these men from the start.[1] "We as a union hated them, because they have damned unions," said Haney. But there was another side to the issue now. The ESOP Committee would have to look at the question of partnering as more than just a management/union issue; as potential owners they would have to consider it as a calculated business proposition. "We were saying, 'this may be the only chance to help the people.' Although, as a union member, I can't stand them." After years of battling this company's management in attempts to organize across the paper industry, partnering with them posed an ethical dilemma. "It's like getting into bed with Satan, but we may have to look at this thing," Haney said in one meeting.[2]

At this point in the meeting, Sutton spoke up, recounting a conversation he had had with Brubaker that might forestall the question. Enso only wanted the Dairy Paks, Sutton said, and so perhaps the union could work a deal with the Swedish company. They could allow Enso to purchase the package and then buy the Canton and Waynesville plants from them. Rose saw this as a very bad business move. The Dairy Paks were the biggest sales base for the Canton and Waynesville plants, and if Sunburst, which was sure to be struggling for operating capital, were to lose control of its primary customer base, there was a good chance it would go under.[3]

Adams brought the discussion back to the question of partnering with the antiunion company. At this point Rose, who, like Adams, had attempted to hold back and allow the committee to make its own decisions, could constrain himself no longer. He expressed "grave concerns about any sort of partnership with [them]." He asked how they could ever hope to win the support of union members if they made such a deal. They had been telling them that the buyout was necessary because if they didn't act someone like this company might come along and buy the mills. "Now we are going to go to them and tell them we are getting into bed with [them]?" he asked. "I hate to tell you this, but it ain't going to fly." When Sutton responded that the partner company would be a minority voice on the board and "couldn't really do any harm," Rose replied that this particular company would "always find a way to get their way. With a nine-member board, the ESOP will probably have three members and the equity investors will have six. Who do you think the majority of the board will listen to," Rose asked, "the ESOP or [the partner company]?"

Sutton allowed that it would be a risk, but perhaps it was a risk that they would be forced to take. Rose, however, would have no part of it. "Don't say I didn't warn you," he said. "You don't understand who you are dealing with. They are making this proposal for one reason and one reason only, for their own self-serving interest." Their offer was not to be taken at face value. "This is highly unusual, for [them] to want to go into partnership with a group of union people. Something just ain't right with this whole scheme."[4]

Focusing strictly on the business aspect of the proposal, Adams brought up the possibility of cutting a deal with the antiunion company, allowing them to buy the package and then purchasing the Canton and Waynesville plants from them. Rose repeated his fear of losing the primary sales base if Sunburst did not control the Dairy Paks. "Without an ironclad long term agreement from the buyer to purchase all of its paper from Sunburst," he said, "the buyer will be adrift in the market. Again, be careful who you go to bed with."[5]

When the meeting broke up, the ESOP Committee and Rose were more uncertain than ever. Not only were they saddled with what had become a moral question, whether or not to partner with a notorious antiunion company, but they were also hearing rumors that Champion itself had invited this company into the bidding process. Still another rumor had it that this company had already placed a bid on its own and was only hedging its bets by contacting Brubaker. ACS was simply advising the ESOP Committee to "sit tight," at the moment, but the committee already had doubts about how much they could trust ACS to keep them informed.[6]

Two days later, ACS moved to push Local 507 closer to a partnership with the antiunion company. Feeling that they couldn't invest any more of their own capital, but fearing that the buyout would fall through if the bid weren't raised, ACS tried to broker a side agreement with Goldman Sachs, the firm that was representing Champion in the sale. L. J. Rose and Bob Smith were at a staff meeting in Richmond, Virginia, when a representative of ACS called requesting permission to send Goldman Sachs a letter saying that the union intended to partner with the company in question. In spite of their opposition to such a partnership, Smith and Rose wanted Local 507's membership to make its own decision in the matter. They instructed ACS to send a carefully worded letter to Goldman Sachs stating that the union was currently considering the proposal, thinking that in the end the local could still have the final say.[7]

The tensions that threatened the solidarity within the ESOP Committee and its relationship with the international began to mount. A few days after the press conference in Canton, which had boosted the community campaign, Rose was back in Canton for an all-day meeting with the ESOP Committee. He went to lunch at the Little Boy Restaurant with Hutch, the new local president, who was having difficulties settling some union grievances. At a nearby table, Rose overheard some Champion supervisors talking. To Rose's horror, the supervisors, who had not been privy to any details of the buyout under the strict terms of the confidentiality agreement, knew "everything about our bidding process, including our original bid, what our next bid was going to be, that [the antiunion company] had gotten into this on Friday and that Enso" was also interested. Rose hurried back to the union hall, where he saw Kenny Sutton and told him what he had heard. At first he was surprised that Sutton seemed unconcerned.

Later, Rose told the story to Gibson, who said that he also had heard a supervisor talking about things he should not have known and that when Gibson asked him where he got his information, the supervisor said that Sutton had told him. Rose was livid. He had been suspicious of Sutton's loyalty and commitment to the union's welfare from the first time he had met with the ESOP Committee. "This is serious," Rose wrote in his daily log. "If Kenny did tell this stuff then we cannot trust him." Rose took the matter to Hutch, who agreed to confront the entire ESOP Committee about the leak the next day.[8]

Sutton noted that Rose had been suspicious of him from the very beginning. "Rose didn't know me from Adam," he said. "I don't think he ever was not suspicious, and I know it was some of my outspokenness. We led the process and I don't think he liked that." And regarding Rose's suspicion that he had leaked confidential information, Sutton said, "I'm sure we all talked. We were under a constant barrage for not being able to share anything with anybody."[9]

Such internal conflicts remained hidden from public view. Back the Buyout was gaining momentum, attracting wider and more diverse support and legitimizing the buyout attempt in the eyes of the public. In early April, one congressional representative, who a week earlier had written to Higgins, "I enthusiastically BACK THE BUYOUT!" made a public show of honoring his promise. North Carolina Republican Representative Charles Taylor invited leaders of the buyout to Washington, D.C., to meet with the state's congressional delegation. The entourage represented the breadth of support that Back the Buyout had attracted. Higgins and Sutton were accompanied by Dale Carroll of Advantage West; Canton Mayor Hardin, co-chair of Back the Buyout; Jack Cecil, president of Biltmore Farms; Mike Wilkins of the state Department of Commerce; Max Lennon, president of Mars Hill College; and Bob Goodale of the Institute at Mars Hill. In the Washington, D.C., meeting, Hardin told Taylor, "Our purpose being here today is to encourage you and other members of the delegation to use whatever is appropriate to urge Champion to deal with our employee group." Taylor, whose earlier statements of support were expansive, now retreated and said that he and the other North Carolina representatives were "not taking a position in the negotiations" because "that would be improper for Congress to do."[10] While the committee had hoped for assistance with fund-raising and legal issues, Higgins noted that Taylor's support had amounted to little more than "allowing his picture to be taken with us."[11] His public comment was nothing more than a compliment of the way Higgins and Sutton had presented themselves: "I can tell you that the presentation the employees have put together is a good one."[12]

Soon after returning from Washington, Higgins and Sutton were off again, this time to New York. As a result of Rose's and Smith's tentative approval for ACS to negotiate with the antiunion company, the ESOP Committee's co-chairs had been invited to meet with officials from both firms. Rose, in Canton to meet with the ESOP Committee, was irritated that the co-chairs were absent from the meeting without his knowledge and complained to the other four members present that he had not been kept well enough informed of the committee's activities. "You either want me involved or not," he told them, "but you will have to make up your minds one way or the other." This time it was Haney who took charge and reassured Rose so that the meeting could proceed. Rose was somewhat appeased by Haney's reassurance that "they definitely wanted me involved as much as possible and that he would talk to them about it."[13]

Nevertheless, Rose was extremely uncomfortable with Sutton in New York negotiating on behalf of the union. He strongly suspected that Sutton had leaked confidential information to supervisors. He had long felt that Sutton put his own personal advancement ahead of the union's interests. And Rose was not alone in his vague suspicion that Sutton may have made promises to outside interests based on his insider knowledge. Sutton seemed just too eager to "do the deal" as quickly as possible, no matter what the costs.[14] "There have been some things that have happened in the last little while that makes me leery of Kenny Sutton and if they prove out to be true, they could be detrimental to the local," Rose wrote in his log. "He does not want me to be involved in the loop on this ESOP. Maybe he feels threatened by me in what, if anything, he is doing. He wants this ESOP to go through at any price and I will not let this happen if it compromises this local or the international union."[15]

In fact, Sutton no longer held fast to traditional concepts of unionism and the union's role in industrial relations, if indeed he ever had. Concepts of worker solidarity and loyalty to the union body over and above the individual are an uncomfortable fit for a man who describes himself as "very vocal and most people either like me or they just fuckin' hate me."[16] It had never been Sutton's way to keep his opinions to himself. "There's not a lot of in between, because I'm not a very passive person. If I think it sucks I'll say it sucks. If I think it's good I'll say it's good." Less than enthusiastic attendance at the union's educational meetings led him to think, "hell, either they ain't concerned, or they don't care, or they're not going to vote for it [to approve the stock ownership contract]." And he was put off by arguments between union representatives at United Auto Workers (UAW), who represented the Morristown, New Jersey, Dairy Pak and those at PACE, his own union.

At the New York meeting, ACS's top officials laid out a plan that called for the potential corporate partner to sweeten the bid significantly and then for the new worker-owned company to split up the package after the deal was closed, giving the partner the Dairy Paks and Sunburst Papers the Canton and Waynesville plants. As part of the deal, the partner company would commit to purchasing a percentage of its raw paper product from Sunburst.[17] Sutton leafed through his copy of the proposal and responded enthusiastically. According to Higgins, he, along with the ACS representatives, "were ready to do the deal right then and there."[18]

But Higgins was skeptical. Somehow the costs in the proposal seemed unrealistic to him. "On a gut level, I just didn't feel like we could do that and survive," he remembered. His gut also cautioned him against cutting a deal with the union's long-time enemy. "Then, there was the whole fox in the hen house thing," Higgins said. He held out, refusing to agree to the deal until the ESOP Committee and the international had a chance for input. "The ACS reps and Kenny were very disappointed in me," he said. "On the plane home, Kenny barely spoke to me."[19]

When Sutton and Higgins returned to Canton, they convened a meeting of the ESOP Committee to report on the meeting with the proposed partner and ACS. Rose arrived just before lunch and found Higgins reporting that Enso was not, after all, interested in being a partner in a bid. Terry Brubaker, Sunburst Paper's recently named CEO, was at the meeting, and he explained that the prospective partner was interested only in operating the Dairy Paks and was willing to invest $100 million in the bid to get them.[20]

Brubaker's selection as CEO represented a good deal of faith on the part of the ESOP Committee. They were keenly aware that they were asking him to do something unique and something that most CEOs would recoil from: share the highest level decision-making power with workers. Gibson explained how the CEO that the worker-owners wanted would have to listen to the new company's "goals and objectives [for giving workers more power over production decisions] and say, 'yeah, I want in on this. This is something different that I've always wanted to do. I don't want to be dictated down to and this would be something I want to be a part of.'"[21]

ACS had chosen Brubaker, but he still had to be interviewed and approved by the ESOP Committee. He had been grilled at length about how he would manage worker-owners, how he would function in an open-book management system, and how he would develop a more cooperative relationship with the union.[22] In this particular meeting, the new workplace culture was tested for the first time. Here was the CEO discussing details of high-level corporate decisions with the worker-owners in their union hall.

Brubaker did listen to the opinions of the potential worker-owners, which by now were knowledgeable and clearly stated. While he gave them their due respect by laying out all of the facts as he understood them, he seemed to favor the proposed partnership with the antiunion company. This company would bring both technical and process expertise to the table, he argued. Furthermore, their expansive knowledge of the industry would provide invaluable knowledge of which specific products should be produced when and for what markets.[23]

Higgins, who had "been in virtually every department—every group in the mill at some time or the other and [had seen] how management treated the employees on the floor," listened to the CEO's arguments with more than a little skepticism. While the company in question had made a priority of fighting unionization, Higgins had come to believe that the workplace fairness that unions represented improved production. "If the employee was treated fairly and was able to use his abilities in the area that he knew best and was treated fairly in the meantime," he later commented, "then everything worked more efficiently."[24]

When Brubaker finished speaking, the committee members laid out their options while Rose took careful notes. They could stand pat with the bid ACS had already submitted. While this would relieve them of their concerns about partnering with an antiunion company, it would leave open the risk of Champion turning down the bid. Champion could then close down the mills or allow them to deteriorate until they were of little value to anyone, leaving nearly sixteen hundred people unemployed. Partnering seemed to be a panacea for all of the financial risks. The jobs would be secure, the long-term debt of the new company would be reduced, and the deal could be closed fairly quickly. The last point alone must have made the proposal tempting to the committee's members, who longed for free evenings and weekends and some semblance of family life. But they felt a loyalty to fellow workers in the Dairy Paks, whom they had brought into the process. "Selling them out" to an antiunion company seemed more like betrayal than a solid business decision. They were also concerned about the public image of their new company. As Rose would say repeatedly, for unionists to partner with a company like the one in question would be "letting the fox into the hen house." There was also the issue of control. As Rose had argued earlier, the partner company would likely use its considerable economic influence over the board to impose its will at every turn.[25]

The prospective partner was anxious for a response. ACS had already told the committee that they expected Champion to call Monday morning, three days away, to find out whether or not they had decided to accept the partnership offer. The committee decided to reconvene early Monday morning and attempt to reach a decision on whether or not to go with this option. It adjourned its Friday meeting on a discordant note. Rose issued another stern warning about "being too hasty in getting in bed with [this company]." He also repeated his concerns that neither he nor Bob Smith had been invited to the previous day's meeting and was not totally convinced by Higgins's explanation that they had tried to get in touch with him.[26] The ESOP Committee broke for the weekend, and Haney (a charter member of Local 507), Higgins (its duly elected recording secretary), Gregg (a vice-president), Henson (who harbored concerns about "an antiunion company coming in here and just busting [the union] and shutting us down"),[27] Gibson (who had eighteen years' experience "in all capacities" of the union),[28] and Sutton (who in spite of his current frustrations with the union had no use for rigid top-down management styles) shuffled out of Local 507's union hall bearing the weight of an entire community's economic health and the integrity of a union that five earlier generations had struggled to build.

On Monday morning, Rose was back at the union hall at 8:00 a.m. to begin an all-day meeting with the ESOP Committee. Ira Wagner and David Steinglass, top-level executives at ACS, arrived around 11:00 a.m., and Bob Smith joined the meeting at 12:30 p.m. After a weekend of what must have been some intense soul searching, the committee set out to clarify all of their options before making a very difficult choice. Steinglass said that he had nothing new to report from the prospective partner or Champion. Then he laid out the options ACS was offering. They could stick with the current $160 million bid. Another possibility was for ACS to submit a $200 million bid with the proposed partner. This company would sweeten the deal by contributing $100 million with the understanding that they would own the Dairy Paks and Sunburst Papers would own the Canton and Waynesville plants. As to concerns about the new company losing its primary market, the partner was willing to commit to purchasing from Sunburst for a period of seven years. If the partner company were left out of the picture, Steinglass suggested that ACS might be willing to raise the bid as high as $180 million.[29]

Smith asked the ACS representatives if they knew of any other legitimate bidders, and Steinglass replied that they were aware of none. Rose then went to the heart of one of the union's biggest concerns. "From what [this partner company] has told you," he asked, "do they intend to possibly shut down some of the Dairy Paks if we sell to them?" The answer was a troubling one for the union. "Yes," Steinglass replied. "Either some of our Dairy Paks or some of theirs or a combination from the two groups. They were not really clear on which ones they had in mind." At this point, the meeting was interrupted by a phone call for Steinglass. When he returned he reported that the prospective partner was eager to go ahead with some kind of agreement. Higgins commented that Champion was expecting a final decision on the bid by the following morning. A critical decision, one that would affect the shape and character of the new company, one that would have a profound impact on how its expanding pool of supporters would view it, would have to be made within twenty-four hours.[30]

Smith spoke up, repeating his reservations. "I have a big problem with turning our backs on the Dairy Paks," he said. They should not be fooled by any offer from this company, who was "into this to make a profit and they will do this any way they can." Smith was for doing "whatever it took to save the Dairy Paks." Steinglass was growing impatient with the union's concerns about the Dairy Pak employees. He was bringing these workers into the realm of international finance, and they were slow to conform to the rules of the game the way it was played at this level. This was purely a business decision for him; there was no room for idealistic considerations of worker solidarity or union protocol. "This group has got to decide if the best business deal is to cut the Dairy Paks loose or not," he said. "We have until tomorrow to make this decision." For Steinglass, the prospective partner's interest afforded an opportunity to smoke Champion out a bit and perhaps find out what their actual bottom line was. "We could tell Champion that we have something with [this company]. This would possibly allow us to learn if the $200 million is reasonable or acceptable. And it would not bind us to [the partner company]."[31]

Smith, a veteran of negotiating with top corporate officials, saw the benefit of exploiting the ambiguity of the situation. He would prefer, though, to play up the long history of enmity between Champion and the proposed partner. He would rather cut a deal with a company he had both battled and bargained with for decades than cut a deal with one whom he did not know well nor trust at all. "Could we not go to Champion and ask them to do some of the financing in order for us to raise our bid and keep [this company] out of the deal?" he asked. "Anything that we do with [this antiunion partner] will be for their benefit and not ours." He was adamant that they should stick to their original purpose, not pushing the deal through at any cost but realizing former local president Mike Coleman's vow to "run any mill we own with respect for people and the environment." "When we started this venture," Smith said, "it was our concern that [this same company] would end up with us [operating the mills.] And now we are talking about joining forces with them!"[32]

Smith's words brought Higgins back to his own vision for the new company. It was a vision that was much broader than how to pad the company's bottom line for the current quarter. It was one in which "the employee . . . was able to use his abilities in the area that he knew best and was treated fairly in the meantime," so that "everything worked more efficiently."[33] In the heated crossfire of what had become a battle for the new company's soul, Higgins's strong, calm voice changed the course of the discussion. "Doesn't it make sense," he asked, "that we talk to each Dairy Pak before we do anything? We did promise them that we would allow them to have input in this venture." "I disagree with that,' Sutton countered. He was finding himself more and more at odds with the union's insistence on protecting its traditional base, dues-paying rank-and-file members. He was, by this time, more sympathetic to Steinglass's argument that they would have to move, and quickly, guided strictly by what was best for business. "I cannot see letting 250 people affect 1,600 people," he said. In his mind, the Dairy Pak workers were tangential to the committee's primary charge. "We were elected to represent the members of Local 507."[34]

Wagner deferred to the union. "If you all want to talk to the Dairy Paks we could probably buy a couple of days more with Champion." At the moment, he felt good about their position. In fact, he thought that perhaps the paper industry's indifference to the sale had them in the driver's seat. "Champion assumed that going into this there were several buyers out there with deep pockets. Fortunately for us, that did not happen." Smith's final words on the matter made his and the international's position clear. "Let me say again, as a member of the international executive board, I cannot support cutting the Dairy

Paks out." And to Sutton's argument that Local 507's interests should predominate, he said, "I owe them support as an executive board member as much as I owe this location." Sutton bristled at the gibe. "I can't see letting the Dairy Paks affect the 1,600 people here at this location. I understand your position and I hope you understand mine." With that, the meeting adjourned so that the committee members could seek input from their assigned contacts in the Dairy Paks.[35]

The following morning, in what seemed like the resumption of one continuous and unending meeting, Higgins reported that only one of the Dairy Paks, Morristown, New Jersey, was in favor of joining forces with the proposed partner. Brubaker, Higgins said, was also leaning toward the partnership option. After more discussion, the committee unanimously voted to refuse the proposal put forth by the antiunion company and let the bid stand as it was.[36]

ACS was not happy with the decision. In a conference call later that afternoon they warned the committee that it was making a "grave mistake." Champion would not accept the current bid, they argued, and they urged the committee to reconsider. Once again the debate resumed, even more heated now. Sutton was eager to talk with the potential partner. Henson agreed that they could talk with them, but stated firmly, "I am not saying to partner with them. I want this to be clear." Higgins reminded the group that they had made a commitment. "When we went into this venture we said that we were going to look after everybody, including the Dairy Paks," he said. "I believe in living up to my commitments. I do not want to get involved with [this company] and sell the Dairy Paks out." He recommended that the committee adjourn so that everyone could contact their assigned Dairy Pak representative and then reconvene the following morning to report on what they had found.[37]

The next morning, Haney, Higgins, Henson, and Gregg all reported that the Dairy Paks were willing to go along with the partnership proposal if the committee could see no other option. However, all had expressed a strong distaste at the prospect. While Rose was reporting on his previous evening's conversation with Bob Smith, reiterating the international's position that it would in no way support a deal with this antiunion company, Higgins was called away to the phone.[38] It was Ira Wagner of ACS. "I'm not supposed to tell you this, Alton," Wagner said, "but you were right about the numbers. If we did the deal that [our prospective partner] proposed, Sunburst would probably be bankrupt within two years."[39] Higgins returned to the table, and with his typical air of quiet respect and assurance simply reported that ACS had changed their minds and decided that they did not favor partnering with the antiunion company. Rose was confounded. "I wonder where they are coming from," he noted. "They change their position from hour to hour."[40]

The committee voted once more. Again, it was unanimous in favor of breaking off relations with the prospective partner, this time with no discussion.[41] It was a moment that Haney would remember as a tremendous relief. He later described the debate over the partnership proposal as the most difficult period of the whole buyout. "We were tickled to death that we didn't do it. [To partner with this company] would just take away from our whole belief or purpose. I mean, we wanted so badly to help everybody, but in doing that, we thought, we'll kill everybody!"[42]

Ira Wagner's optimism that the ESOP Committee and Local 507 were building a winning hand was mirrored publicly by the Back the Buyout campaign. Chris Just was functioning as point man, coordinating the efforts of Price McNabb, the Institute at Mars Hill, and other community supporters. He maintained close contact with the day-to-day work of the ESOP Committee so that public statements would be accurate and, most important, would support, rather than hinder, the intense financial dealings taking place. Just was aware of the proposal to bring the antiunion company into the deal and was prepared to make it clear to the general public, should this come about, that their involvement would be short lived; they were taking only the Dairy Paks and would exert no direct control over Canton and Waynesville. He was also aware that in just two weeks, somewhere around the third week of April, Champion would either accept or reject the final bid, whatever it turned out to be. Just knew that this was the home stretch; there were only two weeks left to put all possible pressure on Champion to accept the bid.[43]

The Back the Buyout Committee was active on many fronts. It had assembled two hundred information packets that included background articles on the history of the buyout, facts and answers to frequently asked questions about ESOPs, and a copy of the new CEO's resume.[44] Price McNabb, with considerable help from Just and Mars Hill College students, had put together a six-page newspaper insert that included an article on Brubaker addressing the question of whether or not a group of workers would have the knowledge and expertise to run a mill, an article by Dan Ray and Mayor C. W. Hardin explaining the tremendous economic impact that the mills' closing would have on the area, and a history of the Sunburst name.[45] Haywood Christian Ministries offered to organize a countywide "Day of Prayer" in support of the union's effort.[46] Ideally, the newspaper insert would coincide with a news conference at the Radisson Hotel in Asheville, as close as possible to the day on which Champion would announce its decision. Unfortunately, Stacy Stafford of Price McNabb learned that the insert could not go into the *Enterprise Mountaineer* until April 30, which could be close to two weeks after Champion's decision on the committee's bid. Nevertheless, due to the uncertain nature of the timeline, he recommended going ahead with it.[47] If the bid had been accepted by that time, the new company would still have a good deal of educating and organizing to do in the months ahead. If it were rejected, the door would still be open for the committee to pursue other possibilities. And, of course, there was no guarantee that Champion would have made its decision on the bid even by April 30.

A meeting of all parties supporting the buyout was scheduled for April 9. Mayor Hardin made the opening remarks, which were followed by an update on the ESOP Committee's progress by Higgins and Sutton. Just and Ray gave a report on the progress of Back the Buyout.[48] The meeting marked a turning point. Instead of being a unifying experience, it led to friction between the ESOP Committee and Dan Ray and the institute. However, it also provided an opening for the committee to step out front and seize a greater control of its own destiny. Just noticed in the April 9 meeting that Ray's initial patient and respectful approach was becoming more "directive, ordering, attempting to take charge." While there was no open, public confrontation at this point, the relationship would only worsen, for while Ray was becoming more directive, the committee was becoming more independent.[49]

The confrontations that were brewing would lead to what Adams would call an educational opportunity for "fostering individual growth and social change, nourishing the fundamental values and complete personal liberty."[50] In short, the men on the committee had learned that the experience and knowledge they had developed made them experts in creating solutions to their own problems. They were creating their own opportunities, controlling their own destiny, and beginning to act without permission. Many were still asking whether a group of factory workers could muster the political wisdom, confidence, creativity, and courage to pull off an international corporate buyout, but the April 15 press conference at the Radisson Hotel in Asheville all but eliminated these voices. The date was carefully chosen; the committee suspected that Champion would either accept their initial bid or reject it before the week was out. They hoped to showcase the impressive coalition of support they had built with environmentalists, government officials, churches, and other unions. The highlight of the press conference was to be the appearance of Terry Brubaker, the new CEO, whose presence and statements of support would underscore the seriousness of the effort.

The Back the Buyout Committee calculated that if Champion were still wavering on the bid, the strong show of community support would make it harder for them to reject it. Champion had carefully crafted an image of "good corporate citizen," and turning its back on this community would seriously tarnish this image. If they intended to accept the bid, the public show of support could only help the next phase, actually setting up and operating an employee-owned company. And if Champion were to reject the bid, a possibility that the committee had already discussed, the buyout attempt would not necessarily be dead in the water; the door would be open to explore other options with a positive boost from the press conference.

Brubaker's appearance would illustrate the new workplace culture. Sunburst Papers would retain the traditional position of CEO, but this particular CEO's "boss" would be the collective body of the worker-owners, and his presence would show his support for the new structure. At first, Brubaker played his new role to perfection. On the day before the press conference, the *Citizen-Times* ran an interview with him in which he commented on the structure and the boss-employee relationship in the new company. The favorable tone and the timing of the article reflected Just's efforts to gain the support of local reporters. "Employees . . . have been steaming ahead with plans to buy Champion's Haywood mills as though there's no chance they won't someday own the mills," it said. Brubaker expressed his delight at the enthusiasm he had noted among the employees. "I would not do it otherwise," he said. "What really got me inspired was the employee enthusiasm. . . . The employees have the know-how and the desire to make it work, and that helps." Brubaker did not hide the fact that the new company faced an uphill battle. The Canton Mill, he said, was "old, it's mid-size, it's expensive to run. And it sits on the Pigeon River, which has become a sort of environmental lightning rod for wastewater discharge issues across the nation." But perhaps he was encouraged by the way that Sunburst's new owners had defused the explosive environmental situation after Champion had failed miserably at it. He added, "You don't really know whether to be optimistic. But the sense of ownership, of not having a boss, will make a big difference."[51]

The day of the Radisson press conference began on an ominous note. A representative of ACS called Local 507's union hall early in the morning to cancel Brubaker's appearance, claiming that he needed to be near his office as the final stages of the bid were being negotiated. "You talk about one pissed off ESOP Committee," remembered Higgins, "but we decided it would be best to just go ahead and cover his ass."[52]

The committee had been closely following news accounts of a story that had broken two days before. The state of North Carolina and Guilford County were attempting to lure Federal Express to locate a huge warehouse and distribution center near Greensboro, in the central part of the state. The state was reportedly offering tax incentives, and Guilford County was prepared to build a sewer line to the proposed site at a cost of over $200,000. Government agencies justified the expenditures on the grounds that the distribution center would create 750 new jobs. ESOP Committee members, and union workers in general, were furious over this. Whereas the hypothetical "new jobs" that FedEx promised were largely part time at subsistence wages, the ESOP Committee and the union had been fighting to keep 1,600 established, good-paying, full-time jobs that supported the local economy with an annual payroll of $87 million. So far the state government had offered them no concrete help.

Kenny Sutton was especially angry over the FedEx issue. Fortunately, in the past six months his political radar had been sharpened to the point that he saw a tremendous public relations opportunity. Without consulting anyone he seized the opportunity, and when his turn came to speak before the sea of reporters and representatives from Governor Hunt's office, he began by quietly thanking the government officials of Haywood and Buncombe counties for their financial support. His next remarks were aimed directly at Governor Hunt's representatives. Reminding the crowd that the governor's office was actively supporting FedEx's efforts with $272 million in incentives, he added dryly, "It would be nice if we had the same resolve in keeping jobs that the state shows in attracting new jobs."[53] "It was brilliant," said Higgins. "Sometimes Kenny would just drop back and throw a long pass when nobody was expecting it. Sometimes we didn't see it coming or the timing wasn't right, and we would just drop the ball. But on this day Kenny threw an eighty-yard touchdown."[54]

When his turn came, Higgins appealed to Champion's stockholders to come out in support of the buyout. "We ask every Champion stockholder to back our buyout by letting Champion know they believe the best and highest return on their investment will be gained by accepting our latest bid," he said. He urged them to cast a vote in support by writing, telephoning, e-mailing, or faxing CEO Richard Olson.[55]

In concluding comments, the political fire that Sutton had kindled was stoked by Buncombe County Commissioner David Young, who had been instrumental in Buncombe's $50,000 contribution to the ESOP Committee. Young underscored Sutton's remarks by commenting that a lot is done to attract new plants, but not much is done to keep the ones already operating. "Do whatever you can to help," he said. "This buyout is tremendous."[56]

It was indeed a touchdown, snatching a stunning victory from the jaws of what had looked like certain defeat. The press conference had been carefully planned so that the public would see the worker-owners and their new boss on the same platform functioning as equals, the old class antagonisms having given way to a new spirit of industrial cooperation. When Brubaker canceled at the last minute, without even the courtesy of calling personally, the committee could have easily fallen back into old patterns of confrontation and blame. Instead, for the good of their new company, the workers chose not only to "cover his ass," but also, following the lead of Sutton's pinpoint political timing, to use their day in the spotlight to pressure the state government to do all it could to support their effort. The general public got the message that even if the CEO didn't show up for work it would be okay; the worker-owners had matters under control at the mill.

Brubaker's cancellation, however, foreshadowed a setback. "ACS had apparently gotten wind of the fact that Champion was going to reject the bid and didn't want his picture taken with a bunch of losers," Higgins said.[57] The morning after the ESOP Committee and the aspiring worker-owners had so successfully grabbed the headlines, Champion snatched them back when the *Citizen-Times* announced "Sunburst Mill Offer Rejected." The article quoted a Champion official as saying, "We were not satisfied with the value of offers that were offered for the Canton facility."[58] Once again, the committee faced a decision about whether to press on or simply accept defeat and wait to see what might transpire.

CHAPTER 8

The Bid Has Been Rejected, Not the Bidders

As the news that Champion had rejected the initial bid leaked into Haywood County, "it was a low," Gibson remembered. "Before the rejection of the bid, you thought, 'Well, there's a chance.' But then afterwards it was a real bad low for a little while because we said, 'We're out. What are we going to do? We've got to do something quick or we're going to lose out on the whole deal.'" At least initially, Gibson wondered if this was the end of the road for the whole effort and possibly for life in Canton as they had known it. "Are we going to do something?" he wondered. "Are we going to be able to get back in it and really be able to contend with it or what?"[1]

The same day that the story appeared in the *Asheville Citizen-Times* and the *Enterprise Mountaineer*, the ESOP Committee gathered at the union hall to take stock. Higgins asked them to think for a minute about what they knew for certain at this point and then waited, poised with a pen and pad to record their thoughts. The responses came slowly and tentatively at first, but then faster, with less despair and resignation and with more confidence and determination. "We decided we weren't going to give up," said Gibson. "We were going to hang together. We were going to see what we could do, one way or the other, to the bitter end."[2]

"As long as Champion intends to sell, Sunburst intends to buy," wrote Higgins. The initial rejection was actually just another step in what they now knew was a very long process. As Higgins noted, it was the bid that had been rejected, not the bidders. "The first bid was just to get us into the second round," explained Gibson. "In other words, you play the first half of the ballgame to get into the second half." Now they were into the second half, and in fact they could point to a number of very hopeful developments. They were confident that their bid had been "pretty reasonably high," and so "we had to assume that we were the highest bidder and that everybody else's bid would have been lower than ours." To expand Gibson's sports metaphor, they had not only survived the first half but also saw themselves as holding a slight lead going into the second half.[3]

They named other hopeful signs. There was the new constructive relationship with environmentalists, which suggested a much brighter future for Sunburst than Champion's history of confrontation. The "Vote-in" campaign, which asked shareholders to phone or fax Champion's corporate offices in support of Sunburst, was gathering strength, and it was "more important now than ever." And they had only just begun to exploit the other theme that the Asheville Radisson press conference had generated. They could increase the pressure on state government by pointing out the short-sightedness of giving economic support to a handful of part-time jobs and only lukewarm verbal support to salvaging the paper mills' $87 million contribution to the region. The chances looked good for gaining a stronger commitment from the governor's office. Higgins made a note to fax both Governor Hunt and CEO Olson informing them that the union was still pursuing the buyout. The atmosphere in the meeting began to build to one of strength and optimism. In spite of Champion's claims that the bid was too low, the committee realized that each day was bringing increased support. "National support from politicians, the faith community, and other employee buyouts," noted Higgins, "is growing, and continued support is being pursued."[4]

Higgins did note one issue that the committee felt would have to be addressed directly and as soon as possible. Champion had always been obscure about its true intentions, giving no real indication of what it considered to be a fair asking price and who, if anyone, had expressed interest in purchasing. The company had even hinted at times that it was in no real hurry to unload the mills. Even the announcement that it was rejecting the bid suggested as much, claiming that "these facilities are making a positive contribution to earnings."[5] What some workers saw as a possibility that Champion might continue to operate the mills indefinitely had always plagued the committee's efforts. While Sutton thought that these people were simply dealing "with things how it makes them comfortable," he had little patience with them. "A lot of people had just as soon not think about" the mill closing. "It's been there since 1908. It's gonna always be there. It's something I don't have to worry about. And they stick their head in their ass or in the sand or whatever, rather than have to come out and face it. And then once it happens they want to blame it on something or somebody."[6]

Haney laughed at the possibility that Champion ever had any real intentions of continuing to operate the mills. Some union members "were saying that Champion never came out and said they'd shut it down. And that's the truth. They never did. They just said that they were going to sell, and that it was there. But not one time did they ever say that they was going to shut it down. And so people took that literally, that if nobody moves we're going to run right on."[7] The committee decided that they would have to force "the issue of Champion's intentions to retain the Canton system or sell the mills."[8] They were certain that Champion had decided to sell to whoever gave them the best offer, be that a "bottom feeder who would run the mills into the ground," until they were forced to close, or the employees, who intended to "run any mill we own with respect for people and the environment." If the choice could be laid out as plainly as this, they believed that much of the opposition to their plans would begin to melt away.

The ESOP's quick and positive response to the rejection was well timed, but it had not come out of the blue. Nearly a month before, they had discussed the possibility and had, at one point, asked Adams for input on how they might proceed should this happen. Characteristically, Adams turned the question back to the committee, asking how they thought they might best proceed. This time, he found that 'the guys were very frustrated at my not making decisions . . . for them. Kenny got so frustrated," he remembered, "that he said, 'I know what your method is, but goddamn it, we need your help and we want you to make a decision for us!'"[9]

It turned out to be one of the rare occasions in which Adams finally did offer advice. In a detailed fax, he advised Sutton and the committee that if the bid were rejected they should move immediately to shift the blame onto Champion, portraying the company as intransigent and unrealistic in its expectations and highlighting the progress the ESOP

Committee had made, their success at putting together a competitive bid, and their laudable vision of creating a company that operated with respect for workers and the environment. The early press releases should express disappointment in Champion's decision but a determination to press on with the effort.[10] As Higgins later put it, Adams urged them to "hop back on that horse we'd just been thrown off and try to ride again."[11]

For their part, the local press cooperated. On April 17, the same day that it ran its headline, "Buyout bids rejected," the *Enterprise Mountaineer* ran a related article titled "Employees regroup after rejection." It led with a quotation from Juanita Dixon of Dixon's Little Boy Restaurant in Canton that conveyed the same dogged determinism that had emerged from the committee. "Any rejection is disappointing for this community, but you regroup and go another way." The remainder of the article reflected the positive points that the committee had listed and worked into a press release. It also suggested that the state of North Carolina was beginning to respond to the committee's appeals. Ronnie James of the North Carolina Department of Commerce commented that keeping the mills open was extremely important to the state's economy and mirrored the committee's efforts to remain upbeat. "I'm disappointed Champion has rejected Sunburst's bid," he said. "But I'm encouraged they've rejected all bids, not just Sunburst's, because it appears the door may still be open." And acting State Commerce Secretary Rick Carlisle, who would later provide critical legislative support, made his strongest public statement to date. His department was working to "keep these good jobs and investment in place in Haywood County" and was "working with Champion and the employee buyout committee to protect the livelihood of these employees and their families." The State of North Carolina backed up the promises of James and Carlisle with a $100,000 grant to the ESOP Committee.[12]

The following week, Gosselin, of Waynesville's *Enterprise Mountaineer*, filed a story that not only reminded the public that the buyout effort was still alive but also, more important, forced Champion to state clearly and unequivocally that it had no intention of operating the mills much longer. It quoted a spokesperson from its central office in

Stamford, Connecticut, as saying, "We haven't heard that [rumor that Champion had changed its mind about selling]." The spokesperson went on to say that Champion intended to "complete the divestiture by the end of the year."[13] In other words, within seven months, according to Champion's spokesperson, the mills might be owned by an unknown corporation, possibly one openly hostile to unions and worker rights or a "bottom feeder" interested only in making a quick profit and then shutting down. Or they just might be owned by the workers themselves. The story laid out the options clearly, just as the ESOP Committee had hoped. Now, perhaps, the public would begin to see that the option they offered was the best, and perhaps the only acceptable, option.

But while the ESOP Committee was redoubling its efforts to buy and operate the mills, Henson recalled that its potential funder, ACS, was advising them to "just sit back and see what happened." In hindsight, Higgins suspected that ACS's enthusiasm had cooled well before the initial bid rejection. He and others felt that the conspicuous absence of CEO Terry Brubaker from the Asheville Radisson press conference was part of ACS's flagging interest in Local 507.[14]

In fact, relations between ACS and the ESOP Committee had been strained for some time. The committee had long felt that ACS was not keeping them well enough informed about their discussions with Champion and Goldman Sachs. Some felt that ACS had attempted to push them into the partnership proposal. Then there was a serious conflict over the amount of the bid, which was not what the committee had understood. To the men on the ESOP Committee, this constituted a serious breach of trust, if not a contract violation. For them, a verbal agreement, between partners no less, carried as much weight as an iron-clad legal document. And when they looked closely at the documents submitted with the bid, they were shocked to find that one of the letters offering financial support quoted a date through which the offer would be good, but that date had already passed by the time that the bid went in! Committee members were beginning to wonder if they should seek funding from another source.

But before proceeding with this, or with anything, for that matter, the ESOP Committee would need the approval of the general union membership. Complicating this was the ongoing problem of the confidentiality agreement, which forbade the sharing of any details about the bid itself or about the contract with ACS. Higgins remembered the options that they took to the union body: "Do we pursue another bid with ACS? Do we get a second opinion from another investment group? Do we do nothing? What direction should we go? But let us give you the details. If we do nothing, the possibility still exists that the mills could be shut down. They could be bought and we could get lower wages from any group that comes in and buys. Or they could be partially shut down by Champion, and only the most efficient, money-making machine or portion of the mill would run. So what do we do here?"[15]

This time around, with Champion's public statement that it intended to unload the mills within seven months, the dangers of doing nothing were more real. Still, when it came to a vote, there were many who felt that the ESOP Committee had had their chance, had failed, and should drop the effort. "We had to bring it to a vote again," continued Higgins. "Do we continue or not? It was a lot narrower margin this time to continue investigations into what made sense. [They told us] either investigate a second bid or get a second option from another group."[16]

With approval from Local 507's membership, the committee decided to begin exploring what other investment groups had to offer. Sutton, who had been in contact with Dan Ray and others at the Mars Hill Institute, used Ray's contacts to arrange a meeting with Bart Fisher and Pat Dowd of Capital House Merchant Banking. Their meeting with the ESOP Committee took place at the union hall on May 6. Rose, who by this point was doubting whether or not they should bother to proceed any further with the buyout, was also at the meeting, along with Adams and Ray.[17]

Fisher and Dowd opened the meeting by assessing the bid that ACS had put forward. They criticized the "quality" of the offer, noting that one potential investor's letter made no firm commitment, and they characterized the other letters of support as "iffy." As the committee had already discovered, one of the letters of intent from a bank had expired on April 1, more than two weeks before Champion turned down the bid. Finally, they saw the $10 million closing fee that ACS required as far too high, confirming what the ESOP Committee suspected. Fisher and Dowd stated without reservation that Capital House was very interested in joining in the venture as the major capital investor. They listed Adm. Elmo Zumwalt, a principal investor, as one of their credentials. Admiral Zumwalt had served as chief of naval operations in the early 1970s and was responsible for the decision to spray the jungles of Vietnam with Agent Orange. After his soldier son had contracted cancer, possibly from exposure to the deadly defoliant, Admiral Zumwalt became an outspoken advocate for environmental responsibility. He had testified against Champion in its battles with environmentalists over the Pigeon River, and Fisher and Dowd thought that having him on the side of the union could be used for public relations. They were confident in their ability to attract long-term customers for Sunburst Papers. And they offered a closing fee that was roughly half of what ACS had required.[18]

Their presentation, up to this point, had been smooth, polished, and professional. No doubt, they believed that they had impressed these hillbilly factory workers, who were dabbling in the world of high finance. But expensive suits, polished presentations, and name-dropping were no longer impressive to the ESOP Committee members, if they ever had been. After many hours of painstaking research, press scrutiny, and meetings with governmental officials, the committee members were not distracted by the glitz; they were focused exclusively on the numbers and other specifics of the proposal itself. So while Fisher and Dowd may have felt that they had made a good impression and could now proceed with the less favorable aspects of their proposal, in fact red flags were popping up among the committee members. They thought that the union might be forced to double the 15 percent reduction in wages and benefits that it had offered. They should forget about having majority ownership, instead giving control to the equity investor and attempting to gain majority control over a period of time. They should also not expect to hire the new company's chief executive and chief financial officers but should leave this choice to the equity investor. They wound up their presentation with the question of "How would you all feel if the equity investor was a foreign investor?" After a pause, Higgins spoke up.

"What about our contract with ACS?" Dowd's response was quick. "Bart can get you out of this." This was too glib of an answer for Higgins, whose father had taught him that "ethical conduct . . . had to be at its height at all times" and that "a man was only as good as his word."[19]

Rose focused on the practical side. "What if ACS sues?" Fisher saw the possibility strictly from a financial perspective. "We would assume that liability," he said. Higgins was concerned about other obligations that would be affected by such a sudden shift. "What kind of reaction would Goldman Sachs have to our changing from ACS to you?" And, of course, anyone who took agreements so lightly would be suspect as a future partner. "What kind of contracts would we have with you?" Higgins asked. The answers were vague, almost evasive.[20] "If you fellows wouldn't mind waiting outside for a few minutes," said Rose, "we have some union business to discuss." Fisher, Dowd, Ray, Adams, and Just all rose to leave, and Rose turned quickly to Adams and Just. "Not you two. You're with us," he said.[21]

While Ray waited in the hall with Fisher and Dowd, the meeting continued. Adams relieved Higgins and Rose's concerns about their agreement with ACS. The firm had already hinted to him that if the committee canceled the contract, they would be "off the hook." In spite of what the committee was coming to see as exorbitant monthly fees, they believed that they had already lost far too much money on the deal. Adams suggested that ACS had already violated the spirit of their agreement, if not the legal contract itself, by not showing the committee a copy of the bid before it was submitted and a copy of the business plan. Furthermore, their service itself had been unsatisfactory, as evidenced by the lack of firm financial commitments in the bid.[22]

But Adams had serious concerns about replacing ACS with Capital House. The idea of allowing the equity investor to name the CEO and CFO ran counter to the model of worker-ownership that the committee had envisioned. What would be the difference in some as-yet-unnamed equity investor deciding who the top officers would be and Champion's board of directors in Stamford, Connecticut, making this decision? It could very well represent a return to business as usual, with the new company controlled by a rigid top-down management structure, its executives chosen strictly on the basis of how well they could pad the bottom line.

Secondly, Adams thought it would be politically foolish to use Admiral Zumwalt for publicity simply because he had testified against Champion in the environmental controversies. Why deliberately antagonize the same corporation that they had finally convinced to take their bid seriously? Champion had already threatened to shut them out of the process once simply because they had gone public with their plans. What could be gained by bringing in a figure who would rekindle the old animosities between Champion and environmentalists?

Rose spoke next. "I personally will not support the foreign investor idea and I am 99 percent sure that Bob Smith will not support this either." The global economy was drawing manufacturing out of the United States as part of a trend that Rose, as a union official, found reprehensible. "These foreign investors are eating our lunch already, and I will not be a part of helping them to destroy us and the rest of the country." Rose agreed with Adams on the issue of allowing the equity investor to select the CEO and CFO. "You are giving up all control of the business," he said. Rose found Capital House's suggestion that the union should plan to concede 20 to 30 percent of its wage and benefit package totally unacceptable and thought that the membership would never accept the idea. "We would have trouble enough selling the 15 percent that we've been looking at," he said. "I am telling you that you will not sell a higher percentage to those employees." He also did not like the idea that they should begin with minority ownership and work gradually toward gaining majority ownership. "Again, you are giving up all control of the business. You cannot do this, and I do not believe that your membership will buy this."[23]

Finally, Rose pointed out the bad timing of the Capital House proposal in terms of upcoming contract negotiations. Capital House wanted to wait until August to prepare the new bid, but the current labor contract was set to expire on August 31. Under the circumstances, Rose was sure that the company would demand major concessions, and he did not feel that the union was strong enough to fight the demands at that time. Higgins questioned this, "Champion is making money, so they probably won't come to us with a concessionary package, will they? They can't do this as long as they're making money." Rose found this hope to be a bit naive. "I'm sorry if you believe that." After all, he reminded them, Champion had put this same money-making plant up for sale. "You only need to look around to see what is happening. Look at what Champion is doing now."[24]

After some more discussion, the committee agreed that there were a number of issues concerning ACS that they needed clear and definite answers on before they took any steps toward what could be a very complicated legal process of dissolving their contract. They wanted to know if ACS still believed that they could bring Champion to the table. Related to this, they wanted to know if they were willing to increase the amount of the bid significantly. With union funds dwindling, and feeling that they had already been overcharged for services, they wanted to know if ACS would be willing to waive fees for any additional service. And, finally, they wanted to know if they would be willing to cancel the contract without a fight if they found these terms unacceptable. The committee took a break while Higgins and Gibson phoned ACS for answers.[25]

Just used the break to check on Ray, who by this time was furious at having been excused from the meeting and was "getting more and more pissed at having to wait." By the time Just came out to check on Ray, he was already in the parking lot about to leave. The final break with the institute would occur a short time later when Ray handed Just a contract that called for the committee to pay a $5,000 fee upfront for the institute's services. The problem, according to Just, was that Ray had earlier made a verbal agreement that the institute would work on a contingency basis, taking only a percentage of the money that it raised. "If the contract had been stamped 'DRAFT,' it might have been different," said Just. But the manner in which Just was asked to present it made it seem both dictatorial and in violation of an earlier agreement. The committee rejected the contract outright, ending its relationship with the institute.[26]

When the committee reconvened, Higgins reported that ACS was still very interested in working with the union, but they would not be able to raise the amount of the bid unless the union would be willing to partner with someone else. Regarding their fees, they said that they were already preparing a letter to the committee stating that they would no longer require consultation fees. The committee agreed that Higgins should tell ACS that they were still interested in buying both the Haywood County mills along with the Dairy Paks, but that they were currently investigating other options.[27]

In spite of the reassurances, ACS and the committee were never again able to function effectively as business partners. So at the end of June, the committee took action. They asked Adams to draft a letter to ACS terminating their agreement. Adams faxed his draft back the same day and the termination letter was sent out the same day by certified mail. ACS replied that they would agree to end the relationship by issuing a letter confirming termination of the agreement. But when the letter came, the committee found it "totally unacceptable." After several more weeks of proposals, counterproposals, threats, and one appeal by Sutton to AFL-CIO President John Sweeny to intervene on their behalf, ACS finally agreed to terminate the contract provided that the committee would sign an agreement not to publicly criticize them or their business practices, an agreement that the committee has firmly honored.[28]

The ESOP Committee was still looking for ways to increase the support of the state government in Raleigh. On their first trip to the capital, Governor Hunt's aid, Joan Weld, had been impressed with Higgins and Sutton. Their sincerity and practical knowledge had moved her and reminded her of why she had gone into public service in the first place.[29] After years of listening to smooth presentations by professional lobbyists, Weld had seen a chance to use her position to better the lives of hard-working citizens. She had been working quietly on their behalf, calling on contacts she had made in her long career in state government.

When the committee's co-chairs returned to the capital seeking government support, Higgins was pleasantly surprised to find that Weld had arranged a meeting with representatives from "the Department of Labor, the Department of Commerce, the tax department and all of that part of the spokes of the political machine that worked through Raleigh." Higgins was deeply appreciative of Weld's efforts, but he also realized that the committee itself had learned a lot about how to build a groundswell of support. "We had to learn the process, learn the ins and outs of the political machine." It reminded him of his job in the paper mill, where he was continually trying to improve the production process. "I adjust and tweak a small part of the process that affects the bigger part of the process. And that's what we had to do, learn that process and tweak a politician here and a politician there and a department of government here and a department of government there."[30]

Higgins and Sutton laid out a broad, comprehensive economic argument that they had developed from researching the economic effects of plant closings and how other states had addressed the problem. In fact, they were likely more knowledgeable about these issues than anyone in the room. "It's not something [government officials] face every day in North Carolina," said Gibson. "After we had done more homework and done more studying on it, [we found that] the state of Ohio has an ESOP Association [built] right into their government. It's part of their Commerce Department. And they use this as a tool to try to keep the industry in the state from going."[31]

The committee had documented the complex interdependence of the local economy of western North Carolina. "We tried to figure out a way to mark every dollar that an employee made at the mill and see how many times it turned over and how many people it would affect down the road," Gibson explained. "You don't think a lot about this, but you get your paycheck over here, and you get it cashed, and you go pay your light bill, and how many people does that payout affect right there? It goes right down the line and [the cash flow] just keeps turning over." Losing an annual payroll of $87 million and throwing hundreds of workers into unemployment would be devastating to the economy of the entire region. "A lot of people who work in this facility live in Buncombe County, . . . and it affects Jackson County because we've got a lot of people who either live out there, or they hunt and fish in the whole western end of the state. So it's a ripple effect, because if they don't have the money to go on vacations, they're not going to be out there at the lake spending money. Or they're not going to be in Buncombe County buying groceries."[32]

This time, the state officials got Gibson's point that "it's not one county versus another county; it's the whole slammin' thing." They could no longer ignore the committee's well-documented argument that the ripple effect would probably spread beyond western North Carolina. "If it affects us here, then it's going to affect everybody on down through the state." At last, state officials began to take concrete action. Governor Hunt, who was still extremely cautious about the legal implications of using his office to show favoritism for one bidder over another, phoned Champion CEO Richard Olson to ask him why the initial bid had been rejected. He reported back to the committee that Champion had simply thought the bid to be too low. In a carefully worded press release, Hunt said that he had urged Champion to keep the interests of the people of western North Carolina in mind, gently implying that Champion should favor the ESOP Committee's next bid. "I want the company to understand the impact their decisions will have on the local economy, and on the livelihoods of the families employed by this company," he said.[33]

While the public support of the governor's office was welcomed, the real practical help came from North Carolina's Department of Commerce, its interim secretary, Rick Carlisle, and Buncombe County's representative, Martin Nesbitt. Adams had worked with Carlisle years before and had urged him to try to find a way to include tax breaks for employee buyouts in Governor Hunt's Economic Opportunity Act. This was the same legislation that the administration was using to attract FedEx to Greensboro, the news of which had provided political fuel for the committee's argument that the state was doing far too little to protect the industry that it already had. Nesbitt stepped forward to insist that the Canton and Waynesville paper workers be named explicitly in the act and that employee buyouts be granted tax breaks as an incentive for keeping existing industry in the state. This alone would free up capital, enabling the committee to raise its second bid on the mills. Nesbitt, with the support of Carlisle, introduced an amendment to the legislation to ensure that it also included employee buyouts.[34]

Carlisle may have been influenced by a conversation with Gibson in which Gibson argued that the state would benefit from the legislation regardless of whether or not Sunburst Papers succeeded. Their effort would provide a new model and could serve as another tool in the state's economic development toolbox. Gibson had assured Carlisle that the ESOP Committee would offer its knowledge and support to any other group of workers in the state who wanted to try what they were doing. The bill, which gave the same job-creation tax credits to employee buyouts that FedEx would get in Greensboro, sailed through the legislature. Carlisle announced that it could benefit Sunburst to the tune of $14 million in tax breaks, virtually assuring that the committee's second bid would be substantially higher.[35]

The committee had scarcely missed a step between the rejection of the initial bid and beginning work on the second bid. On May 13, immediately after the union body had given its approval, Alton Higgins had written to both Olson and Bob Higgins of Goldman Sachs on behalf of the ESOP Committee indicating their intention "to submit a second Letter of Intent to Purchase assets of the Canton System on or before August 15, 1998."[36] This time around the committee's experience would come into play from the beginning. They knew the due diligence that would be required for a second bid and they knew how to carry out the process. They knew what the mills were worth on the market, what Champion was hoping for, and they had a sense of what they would be willing to settle for. Perhaps most important, they were now clear and confident about how they intended to operate, both as a committee and later as an employee-owned company. They intended to be owners in fact, not just in name. They would make their own decisions, in collaboration with other workers in the plant. They would simply choose not to work with consultants or investment bankers who tried to dictate to them or to shut them out of the decision-making process.

After severing its relationship with ACS and refusing the offer of Capital House, the ESOP Committee found itself pursuing a buyout with no funder, until Bob Smith, the union's international vice-president, brought in KPS Special Situations Fund of New York City for discussions.[37] From the beginning, many things about KPS appealed to both the international and the ESOP Committee. From its recent experiences, the committee had become skeptical of outside offers of help, and when KPS representatives David Shapiro and Mike Psaros walked into the union hall the first time, they were put through an informal test. According to Just, Sutton turned to one of the representatives, who obviously had not bought his clothes in Canton, and said, "I'm not sure I can trust a man wearing a pink shirt." The KPS people passed the test with quick, good-natured comebacks. On a more serious note, they made it clear that they wanted open communication directly with the committee members at all times. They gave their cell phone numbers to every committee member and urged them to call at any time. They thought it absurd that ACS had asked for such a large monthly payment and assured the committee that their firm would receive nothing until the deal went through. To show their sincerity, they offered to fly Sutton and Higgins to New York to meet with more members of their staff.[38]

At last, the ESOP Committee appeared to have found a funding partner that felt like a good fit. In the terms of Henson's metaphor, the committee had finished the first half in good shape and had opened the second by scoring a goal.

CHAPTER 9

Up against the Wall

Relations on the shop floor grew more tense and uncertain. In May, a meeting between Hutchinson, Rose, and local management representatives turned confrontational. The union reps were concerned about the number of temporary workers Champion had brought into the mill at the same time that there was talk of downsizing in certain departments. Hutch and Rose were skeptical of management's claim that the company was only trying to streamline by consolidating all of its temp contracts with one agency.[1]

Rose asked why the company had not agreed to a hearing date for a particular grievance, and the confrontation escalated into threats. The managers claimed that they had the right to hear grievances in the order in which they had been filed, and the union men countered that as the party bringing the grievance, they had the right to decide which grievances would be dealt with first. Rose accused the managers of retaliating against the union for a similar grievance the previous year, and when the managers refused to relent, Rose promised that the union would "go to battle" over the issue. The number of grievances had been steadily mounting in recent years, but now it soared. With the fate of the mills still up in the air, managers and workers were tense, irritable, and defensive.[2]

On the same day that Rose and Hutch were battling management over grievance procedures, Higgins formalized the ESOP Committee's intent to submit a second bid with letters to Goldman, Sachs, and Champion's CEO, Olson. Speaking on behalf of the ESOP Committee and "all employees in the Canton system," Higgins committed to a three-month deadline, promising that the second bid would come "on or before August 15, 1998."[3] One reason for the sense of urgency and the short time frame was financial. "We were just about out of money," said Gregg. "Union funds had just about run out. We were just about up against the wall without having any more feasible options out there."[4] As always, the ESOP Committee was concerned about maintaining the tenuous support it had won from the union's general membership. Not only were the uncertainties heightening the tensions between management and labor, they were also fueling conflicts within the union. Whenever possible, the committee attempted to bring the facts, as they understood them, back to the membership. Higgins outlined their argument: "If we do nothing, the possibility still exists that it could be shut down. The possibility still exists that it could be bought and we get lower wages from any group that comes in and buys. Or it could be partially shut down by Champion, and only the most efficient, money-making machine or portion of the mill would run. So, what do we do here? And we tried to explain to the groups [of employees] that we talked to what the outcome could be."[5]

Another reason for the three-month deadline was the fact that Local 507's contract with Champion was due to expire on August 31. As things stood, the union would enter negotiations with little bargaining leverage. If Champion only intended to operate the mills until it could "get full value price for the operations," as it was saying publicly, it had little incentive to make concessions to the union.[6] And with the union's treasury nearly depleted, it would be difficult to mount a publicity campaign or use any threat of a strike.

Champion's much maligned environmental record raised a legal issue for Sunburst Papers. It was unclear how much liability the new company would assume for the environmental problems created by the previous owner, and the ESOP Committee again turned to the state of North Carolina for assistance. Working with John Runkle, the environmental lawyer it had hired as a consultant, the committee explored the possibility of obtaining a Brownfields Agreement with the North Carolina Department of Environment and Natural Resources (DENR).[7] Under a Brownfields, the DENR would lay out the required cleanup and land management goals, and as long as Sunburst met them the state would grant them liability protection. Such legal protection would make the new company much more appealing to potential investors.

The Brownfields letter of intent promised a new approach to environmental issues. Sunburst was committed to capital investments in environmental improvements that would "benefit the public through significant contaminant reduction, or near-elimination of containment emission in the air, the water and the soil." The letter then out-lined the Sunburst environmental philosophy. With the "official sup-port of environmentalists," the worker-owners would "find ways to earn high marks from all interested organizations and agencies for an open approach and strong focus on environmental performance." As potential owners, they vowed "to hold managers to this goal, mea-suring their performance and compensation accordingly."[8]

Runkle found that none of the areas around the Canton or Waynesville mills would qualify for protection under a Brownfields Agreement. He did, however, recommend that Sunburst take steps to protect itself from liabilities for conditions created under Champion's ownership. He advised the ESOP Committee to hire an environ-mental engineering team to do extensive studies before the buyout was finalized, so that potential problems could be uncovered and the cleanup costs could be factored into the purchase price. Champion could then be required to clean them up before the sale or could make a legal agreement with the state to clean up environmental haz-ards in exchange for protection from future liabilities.[9]

Runkle was most concerned about the three landfills located along the Pigeon River where Champion had dumped dioxin-filled sludge for decades. These were the same landfills that had raised the ire of environmentalists and Tennessee landowners, who had charged that this dioxin had seeped into the groundwater and caused higher levels of cancer. The landfills had already been the basis for several lawsuits, both against Champion and against the state of North Carolina, and Runkle strongly recommended that the purchase agree-ment exclude these sites. He could see no real problems with the pre-sent landfill that Champion was using and suggested that the ESOP Committee find out how long it was expected to be usable and con-sider purchasing additional land for landfills, as property values in the area were steadily increasing. Runkle noted several improvements in water quality and monitoring procedures by Champion and rec-ommended that the company be required to disclose all of the results of its monitoring program.[10]

A lingering problem for the ESOP Committee was the contract with ACS which had still not been officially dissolved. The major sticking point was ACS's claim that it was due a percentage at closing even if it were no longer representing Local 507. Bob Deutsche, the union's attorney, was looking at the matter and was considering the possibility of a suit.[11] The ESOP Committee learned of a conflict between the AFL-CIO and ACS. David Gladstone, a salaried chairman and a major stockholder of ACS, was also president of the Coastal Berry Company of California. Coastal Berry was locked in a struggle with its employees, who were seeking to affiliate with the United Farm Workers, and some organizers claimed that it had launched an intimidation campaign against the workers. John Sweeney, the AFL-CIO's national president, had written Malon Wilkus, ACS's president and CEO, about the "damage" that was being done to their relationship. "We recognize that ACS has worked very hard for unions and their members," wrote Sweeney. "We would like very much for this work to be able to continue. But, like all of the labor movement's relationships, this work must rest on a common respect for the rights of workers."[12] The ESOP Committee saw an opportunity to enlist the help of the AFL-CIO in terminating their contract with ACS. Sutton wrote Sweeney on behalf of the committee, seeking "input regarding our predicament and any other helpful influence you might offer on our behalf."[13]

On August 5, Higgins, Hutchinson, and Rose held a conference call with Mike Psaros and David Shapiro of KPS, Mike Correy from Champion's home office, and Marc Nachman of Goldman Sachs. Champion aired its concerns and complaints, and Psaros and Shapiro were able to address them directly. The discussion was open and frank. Psaros assured the Champion and Goldman Sachs representatives that their letter of intent "was a sincere one and that we have no intention of doing what ACS did in their bid submission." Correy took this cue to lay out a host of complaints that Champion had about the way ACS had performed. For starters, the bid had been far too small. ACS had "complained constantly about our being slow on getting to them some of the requested information." They had only been trying to document the accuracy of the information they provided, Correy claimed.[14]

Correy charged that workers in the Canton and Waynesville mills had made threats to managers about "what they were going to do to them once they bought the mill." He repeated the company's concerns about the amount of news coverage, claiming that it had "the potential to impact our customers." With the extensive news coverage, "some amount of confidentiality was compromised during the process also." The ESOP Committee members shared many of Champion's frustrations with ACS. The disagreement over the amount of the bid had marked the beginning of the end of the committee's partnership with ACS. "And from there on it went downhill with that group," Gregg said.[15]

It was not unlikely that some hourly employees had threatened to seek revenge once they became owners. This had become, after all, a tense and mistrustful workplace culture where workers felt that the company had violated both the spirit and the letter of their 1990 cooperative contract negotiations. Since that time, grievances had skyrocketed and management was often viewed as "outsiders" and adversaries. But such talk could hardly be avoided. As Higgins said, "Shop talk prevails and there is nothing we can do about this." Champion should have no concerns about the ESOP Committee or anyone that it took into official confidence, though. "We know and recognize the importance of confidentiality," Higgins said, "and [we] try hard to maintain this confidentiality at all times."[16]

The media was another matter. As Haney said, the ESOP Committee was "in a real quagmire" here.[17] Higgins explained that the committee knew it could not pull off the deal without support from the local community and government agencies, and it was "almost impossible" to win and maintain this support without the news media. As Higgins said to Correy and Nachman during the conference call, "we have some politicians involved in some legislation and grants and they want some limelight. Is this a problem with you all?" Correy replied only that "timing is important. Champion does not want any press coverage nor any limelight. This could be disruptive to the process."[18]

Psaros sought to reassure the Champion and Goldman Sachs representatives that the amount of the bid would likely rise after they had done their due diligence. Nachman countered that ACS "told us the same thing that you are telling us now about possibly raising the bid at some time and this is a big concern to us. We heard this before." But KPS was simply trying to be "realistic and up front," said Psaros. "We would not be spending thousands of our dollars if we were not sincere. If we can't reach your expectations, we will tell you so," he said. Correy seemed somewhat reassured. He even suggested a way to deal with the problem of the tension and mistrust between managers and workers that had plagued both sides during the previous negotiations. "It may help if we brief our salary people in the plants," he suggested. "Maybe we should allow you all to talk with key management first.[19]

The conference call ended on a positive note, with Correy promising that Champion would provide them with their best people for these discussions and give them anything they requested. And, in spite of the fact that Olson, Champion's CEO, and Kenwood Nichols, its vice-chairman, were "concerned about the gap" between the initial bid figures and what the company expected to get, Correy expressed hope that Champion's board of directors would "say go ahead with this." He promised to report back to the ESOP Committee by the end of the week.[20]

This crack in the icy relationship between the ESOP Committee and Champion's corporate board came at a critical time for the union, which was literally at the end of its labor contract. If the fate of the mills remained uncertain, the union could not even be sure who it would be negotiating with. Even with the likelihood of a successful buyout, contract negotiations would still be problematic. As owners, the workers would have to be as concerned about the long-term stability of the company as they were about increasing salaries and protecting benefits. In addition, the contract would be with KPS, its primary capital provider and, at least for the foreseeable future, part owner of the new company.

With all of these uncertainties, the ESOP Committee desperately wanted one thing in the new contract that the union had never had before, a successor clause stating that if the company were sold the new owners would be obligated to honor the existing union contract. This would provide protection for the workers should the new company falter and be forced to sell. As a practical matter, it would also be a strong selling point when the ESOP Committee sought approval of the new contract from the rank and file.[21]

When Olson and Nichols heard the account of the conference call with KPS, they requested a meeting with representatives from the ESOP Committee and KPS at their corporate headquarters in Stamford,

Connecticut, and a second meeting with Goldman Sachs in New York City. Higgins and Sutton attended the meetings and reported to the full ESOP Committee that they had gone very smoothly and were much more open than past meetings. Goldman Sachs had gone so far as to admit that Local 507 was currently the only potential buyer of the Canton system. Higgins and Sutton believed that Champion and Goldman Sachs were "more than willing now to help us in finalizing a deal."[22]

The New York meetings were a turning point. Champion and the ESOP Committee, backed by KPS, were now working together toward making the buyout happen rather than confronting each other with accusations. They were committed to sharing information rather than keeping secrets. The ESOP Committee could now operate under the assumption that the deal was going to go through and could turn to fine-tuning all of the many details that would have to be addressed in the coming months.

The issue of how to legally sever its relationship with ACS still plagued the ESOP Committee. Bob Deutsch, Local 507's attorney, was present at the meeting in which Higgins and Sutton reported on their New York trip and spoke to the matter. Deutsch advised sending ACS a letter proposing a mutual termination of the agreement. If they refused, Deutsch was for proceeding immediately to the courts. Deutsch noted that the ESOP Committee, not Local 507 or the international, had signed the contract with ACS. So one legal maneuver would simply be to disband the committee. Since it had no assets, ACS would have no incentive to take it to court. Deutsch also noted that the contract had a binding arbitration clause, so if the committee were to take the case to the courts it could possibly win something through this.[23] Another option was to argue in court that ACS had already terminated the contract through an earlier comment that they had "done all they could for you on this transaction." A final option might be to do nothing until the deal went through with KPS and then offer ACS $50,000 as a settlement. The committee deferred the decision for a while longer, still hoping that ACS would honor its earlier statement that it would voluntarily terminate the agreement.

Another extremely sensitive issue surfaced at this meeting. It concerned the committee's relationship with SACCO and what percentage

SACCO would be paid after the deal went through. With Adams and Just present in the meeting, Sutton reported that KPS was "very much concerned" with SACCO's proposal that they receive 4 percent of the purchase price and instead favored a flat payment of $250,000. According to Sutton, KPS felt that the 4 percent figure was "way out of line" compared to the 2 percent that they were receiving for "putting everything together, including the financing, plus all of the money that they are putting into this of their own."[24] If Adams felt any personal affront, he covered it tactfully. "We do not want to come across as being greedy," he said, "and we only want what is fair." He reminded the committee that in the end, SACCO would only get 2 percent of the closing costs, with 1 percent set aside for "educational purposes" and another 1 percent set aside for dealing with "environmental issues," two areas that would have to be developed if the new company were to survive and develop a more democratic workplace culture.[25] As Adams explained later, "Every business situation is different. It has a different culture, a different dynamic and . . . there's a history of the way people do things in that business, that, in effect . . . upsets traditional power relationships." Adams knew that the educational funds would be necessary for developing this new culture.[26]

Just attempted to put their fee in context, reminding the committee that SACCO had been instrumental in securing private funding, government funding, and tax incentives. Realizing that the committee would probably feel constrained discussing the matter in front of him and Adams, Just suggested that they step out while the committee held a private discussion. When they were alone, the committee quickly agreed that 4 percent of the purchase price was too much to give SACCO. KPS had worked hard on their behalf and on top of that was putting their own money into the deal, knowing that they stood to lose it if the deal fell through. As Rose summarized the argument in his notes, SACCO "had only invested some time and have been compensated for most of this," and giving them 4 percent at closing would constitute "a slap in the face to KPS."[27]

Sutton had questioned SACCO's motives and value to the committee for some time. While taking pains to explain that he considered Adams to be a personal friend, he later said that he was "disappointed in Frank's motives . . . because I felt like Frank was looking for something, kind of, that would put SACCO on the map. And that he was more in it for money than what I thought he was in the beginning." According to Sutton, SACCO's contribution had been minimal, and KPS was aware of this. "Matter of fact, there was lots of conversations from KPS, 'why are you paying Adams anything? When you guys are doing all the work.'" Sutton acknowledged that paying SACCO was "the right thing to do because we said we'd do it," but still said, "I'm not sure the value was there." Just took exception to Sutton's downplaying of SACCO's role, believing that the buyout effort would never have begun without SACCO and that he and Adams had "guided the whole process."[28]

With Adams and Just waiting out in the hall, the committee began to see that there would continue to be unforeseen costs at closing and after. They decided to set up a discretionary fund of 1 percent of the sale price, which could be used by the ESOP Committee to pay for "certain items pertaining to the buyout." They would use part of these funds to pay SACCO a flat fee for services provided, instead of the 2 percent with 2 percent more for environmental issues and education that SACCO had proposed.[29]

After the meetings in Stamford and New York, it was clear to most everyone that the ESOP Committee, with KPS as principal funder, was about to make an offer that Champion would accept. But there were many issues yet to be resolved: What percentage of stock would the employees own through their ESOP? How much of a voice would workers have in the hiring of the new CEO, CFO, and mill manager? How much of a voice would they have in operating the mills? One of the stickiest issues would be the role of the union in the new company. In effect, these union workers would be responsible for writing their own contract and getting it ratified by the rank and file, a quite different role from the traditional adversarial relationship between management and labor. Would they recommend a wage or benefit cut? Could they, as loyal union members, in good conscience recommend to their fellow workers that they vote for a concessionary contract? How could they sell such a contract to the union membership, many of whom harbored deep suspicions of their motives?

The committee laid out a plan to get a commitment from KPS on the key issues and then to hold a series of informational meetings with union members and their families. They knew that they would have a difficult time overcoming the mistrust months of imposed silence and evasive answers had engendered. They also knew that they could neither complete the deal nor operate Sunburst Papers as an employee-owned business without rank-and-file support.

There had been some discussions between the committee and KPS on who would hire company officers and managers, what percentage of stock the employees would own in the new company, and what profit sharing would look like, but now, before beginning the process of educating workers and their families about the contract they were voting on, the committee wanted something in writing. KPS proposed that the union adopt a seven-year contract with Sunburst that would include a 15 percent reduction in some combination of wages and benefits for both hourly and salaried employees. KPS also noted that it expected productivity to rise, as was ordinarily the case with employee-owned businesses, and thus the new company should require fewer employees. However, KPS's proposal did note that it expected to be able to meet the need for fewer employees through attrition and voluntary early retirement.[30]

In theory, the 15 percent reduction could be minimized through profit sharing. Sunburst would set aside 10 percent of its annual pre-tax income to be divided up among salaried and hourly employees. So if the employees were productive, and if the market were strong, the thinking went, the employees could regain their 15 percent concession and more. The employees would own 40 percent of the common equity stock, with KPS retaining 55 percent. The new company's senior management team would be offered the remaining 5 percent. KPS would make a cash equity investment of $30 to $40 million, and in order to help protect this investment, would retain the same value in preferred stock, which it could collect on only if the company were sold or failed. Sunburst's board of directors would include eleven members, the CEO, three chosen by the union, one by the salaried employees, and six by KPS. Each board committee would be required to include at least one of the union-designated directors. Immediately after closing, a reengineering task force with three senior managers, three union representatives, and a representative of KPS would be appointed by the board. This task force would study management culture, workplace organization, and company policy and would report to a special committee of the board. KPS wanted to retain the right to sell all or any part of its interests in Sunburst, but it would agree to notify the union thirty days before notifying any other prospective buyer. In the matter of hiring top management, KPS would give the union the "opportunity to meet and interview 'short list' candidates for the Company's Chief Executive Officer" and would "give serious consideration to the Union's views concerning such candidates."[31]

Robert Deutsch studied KPS's proposed terms and faxed a response to Higgins and the committee. He requested that KPS be more specific about reductions in the workforce, while avoiding numbers, and he felt that the language should stress that this would be accomplished through "natural attrition." The preferred stock provision troubled Deutsch some because, should the company be sold or go public, "the ESOP could *effectively own* substantially less than 40% of the equity."[32] Deutsch noted that under the KPS proposal the union would not have first right of refusal if KPS decided to sell. He saw a potential problem here in that "KPS could sell out to a group the union does not feel it is able to work with, and there is nothing the union could do about it." However, looking at the matter practically, Deutsch did not think it likely that KPS would sell its interest. The ESOP structure itself would provide some measure of protection here. "It is unlikely that a potential purchaser would buy KPS out if the union is not at least in a cooperative mode, since your enthusiastic cooperation is vital to the future success of the company." And while the union would have no legally protected first right of refusal, Deutsch was convinced that KPS was committed to notifying the union first if it was considering selling, so that the union would have an opportunity to purchase KPS's interest.[33]

Three days later, the ESOP Committee signed the term sheet agreement. It formalized what Higgins referred to as "sacred issues," things that the committee had been committed to from the beginning. The first of these sacred issues was profit sharing. The agreement specified that the company would contribute 10 percent of its pretax income to a profit-sharing plan for employees. It also specified that the contract should contain language incorporating the ESOP structure and that the board would establish a reengineering task force to study and recommend changes in management culture and workplace organization.

Later, the committee had additional concerns about the new company and expressed them in a memo to KPS. They wanted more than a chance to "interview 'short list' candidates for the Company's Chief Executive Officer." This was one of the most critical decisions that would affect the viability of Sunburst, and if the new company were to be democratic and employee-owned in fact, they wanted more input in these matters. "The employees feel that the future success of the Canton system is directly related to the hiring of new senior management including but not limited to the CEO, the CFO, the Mill Manager, the Director of the Dairy Paks and the Assistant Superintendent of Maintenance," they wrote. Also related to personnel, the Canton employees, through the ESOP Committee, "respectfully request[ed] a voice in making . . . decisions" about which positions would be eliminated and which would be retained. The ESOP Committee also requested that KPS consider purchasing control over the water rights of Lake Logan to ensure an ample water supply for the facility and that it develop a long-term replacement plan for the lime kiln that was currently being used. The committee anticipated that the union's information sessions would cost time and money and that there would be other costs associated with closing. They requested that KPS cover these costs.[34]

There were other issues that the ESOP Committee wanted to see addressed, including retirement benefits, details of a 401K plan, health insurance, and the Service Awards Program, through which Champion had rewarded employees for every five years of service. Finally, the issue of where the corporate headquarters would be located was a critical issue. "The location of the new company's headquarters in Western North Carolina is an issue that is very important to us, as it is to many residents of this area," they wrote. "The ESOP Committee expects to play an active role in the decision of where the corporate headquarters are located."[35]

Winning approval from the Dairy Paks was critical. These packaging plants formed a symbiotic relationship with the Haywood County mills, turning the paper produced into a key marketable commodity, juice and milk cartons, while depending on the Haywood mills for the paper needed to create that product. They were scattered in six different states, and while five of the six Dairy Paks were represented by PACE, they had little direct contact with Smoky Mountain Local 507, except when it was time to negotiate and vote on a new contract. The sixth, located in Morristown, New Jersey, was represented by a different international, United Auto Workers. While the lines of communication were tenuous within Local 507, they were nearly nonexistent with the Dairy Paks. And yet when it came time to vote on the contract, which would include approval of the formation of Sunburst Papers as an ESOP, their votes would carry the same weight as those in Canton and Waynesville. Clearly, the ESOP Committee would have to do some serious and intense political bridge building to get the Dairy Paks on board.[36]

Sutton, who was the primary contact for the Dairy Paks, described what amounted to a turf war between the UAW and PACE in Morristown. "It was like two men pissing over a post to see who could piss the highest. It was a union thing; UAW didn't want PACE telling them what to do and PACE wasn't going to go in and run across those lines, those sacred lines. So we, as a committee, hadn't had the opportunity to talk with the UAW folks."[37] In mid-October, the ESOP Committee hosted a three-day conference for representatives from the Dairy Paks to explain what an ESOP was, to unveil the particulars of the plan they were working on with KPS and where the Dairy Paks fit into the plan, and to answer questions.[38]

Sutton set out on a mission to update the Dairy Paks, sound out their concerns, and bring them on board to ratify the contract when it came up for a vote. He visited Dairy Paks in Georgia, Iowa, Texas, New Jersey, and Olmsted Falls, Ohio, where he had "seen some issues." Pete Dagostino, the local president in Olmsted Falls, had assured Sutton that a majority was in favor of the buyout. Still, when he reported on the buyout's progress to his membership, Dagostino stopped short of an outright endorsement. He stuck to the facts, laid out the profit-sharing plan, and noted that there didn't appear to be any other interested buyers. He commented that Champion seemed to have stopped investing in the Canton system, which suggested that they were serious about selling. Without specifying numbers, Dagostino told the local's members that there would likely be reductions in wages and benefits. He pointed out that they would be expected to increase productivity, that the workforce would likely be reduced, and that work procedures and rules would likely change. He made it clear that he was not taking a position either for or against the buyout. "I in no way mean for this letter or anything else I say to influence your vote. I am only passing on the information I was given."[39]

Sutton began to sense that his efforts were paying off and that the Dairy Paks were slowly coming on board, though some were still uncertain: "Fort Worth, from Robert Blake [local president] and his guys . . . kept saying that there wasn't a lot of issues with it there. . . . Clinton, Iowa was a hundred percent for it because they were slated to be shut down. If this deal didn't go through and Champion kept them, they were gonna shut them down. So they knew that they were going down, that this was their only option. So we knew they were for it. I had a great meeting with Clinton, nobody was out of the way."[40]

The ESOP Committee made the first public disclosure that they, KPS, and Champion had reached a price agreement in a conciliatory letter to all employees of the Canton system. "We are aware of the anxiety and frustration that you and members of your family have experienced over the past year," it began. "We hope that you understand that Champion required that the ESOP Research Committee and their advisors sign a strict confidentiality agreement which severely limited our ability to communicate with you during the last year." This regrettable situation, the letter promised, was about to change. "We are now able to talk more openly about the buyout effort and intend to do so at the upcoming Information Meetings." The letter listed eleven "advantages of an ESOP," which emphasized greater employee input and more amiable relations between management and employees. The final advantage addressed what was probably the most important concern for everyone in the Canton system, job security. After a year of uncertainty as to who, if anyone, would own and operate the mills, the committee held out the possibility that employees could achieve security through controlling their own destiny. The informational letter also listed a series of questions that would be covered at the upcoming information meetings which mainly concerned how profit sharing would work, what form the new contract would take, what wages and benefits would be like, and such specific concerns as who would be the CEO and where the corporate office would be.[41]

Doug Gibson was relieved finally to be able to share all of the details of the buyout, believing that sharing some facts while withholding other information had done more harm than good. "If you come out there today and give me a small little piece of it, that's going to get me really going. 'Well you said you were going to tell us all of it, now you just give us a little piece. That all you can give us?' And it would disrupt your people so bad." Gibson explained the rationale for holding a series of information meetings on selected topics. They would hold meetings that would "give them this much, they can comprehend that much in that meeting. Then we'll have another meeting and we'll give them some more of it. We'll have another meeting and we'll give them another section of it. Then some more, and we actually stepped it off as to what our plan was. We planned it out, [to first give them] the financial. Then we'll give them the business side, the contract side, we'll give them all of it and we'll just piece it all together as it goes down, and that's basically what we had to do."[42]

Champion was much more open with KPS than it had been with ACS, but the company still preferred to operate as quietly as possible and maintain control of the process. Higgins commented, "We had been finally getting the opportunity to start holding these meetings. And still, Champion [only] allowed us to have conversation with three managers." And while they were much freer to talk, Champion still insisted that they stick to generalities.

> We really weren't able to discuss a lot of the details with the managers until right up at the end of April, first of May and still only in a general fashion, not in real details. We had the ability to discuss more details with the contract and issues and benefits and so forth with the union in smaller groups. There was just meeting after meeting after meeting to discuss business plans, details of what would be in the contract, what would be in the ESOP, the whole aspect of what concession, investment, meant, what proportion and the

whole profit sharing details, stock ownership details, the whole menagerie of things and the details that had to be worked out.[43]

Champion's reluctance to allow the ESOP Committee to discuss details with managers also made it nearly impossible to begin negotiating a contract. This was frustrating for KPS, which was attempting to finalize investment plans. According to Higgins, KPS told the committee, "Well, we have to have a contract, you have to have a contract to vote on which incorporates ESOP as part of it, which incorporates ownership as part of it, which incorporates profit sharing and incorporates the reduction in wages and benefits." Since it was Champion who was imposing the strict confidentiality standards, the committee decided to ask them for help from a company human resources expert in writing the contract, "and Champion refused to do that."[44]

KPS finally turned to the ESOP Committee itself, telling them, "Well, we don't have an attorney that knows anything about writing union contracts. You write your own union contract that incorporates the 15 percent reduction in wages and benefits and doesn't raise the cost of that contract over a seven-year period." This added yet another responsibility to the tremendous burden that the ESOP Committee already carried and another round of on-the-job training. "Can you imagine? This whole concept that we've been used to, of negotiating a contract between the company and the union—and the union is given the ability to write their own contract," said Higgins.[45]

By the first week of December, a handshake agreement had been reached between Champion, the ESOP Committee, and KPS. Deutsch was working on the legal aspects of "transition issues." He encouraged the committee to press Champion to reduce management positions as much as possible so that this would not be one of the first actions that Sunburst would have to perform. He advised that Champion should provide all the documents about the plant and its operations that it had and that it should do most of the removal of old electrical wires and machinery. Champion should identify all of its old landfills, along with a complete accounting of what materials were buried in them. To ease the business aspects of the company's first few months of existence, Champion should seek "handoff" agreements with suppliers that would, as far as possible, preserve the already existing supplier agreements. A date should be specified until which Champion should be responsible for workers' compensation claims.[46]

Deutsch raised the issue of the water and easement rights around Lake Logan, saying that they needed to be clarified. And, finally, he encouraged them to seek some more specific information that had been promised from KPS on how best to continue providing employee benefits, a critical issue in the upcoming contract negotiations.[47] One rumor flying around the mills was that the union would be forced to accept whatever contract the committee came up with, without a vote by members. The rank-and-file's mistrust and suspicions were understandable. They had learned through the media that Champion had put them up for sale, and for a year the ESOP Committee, under the constraints of the confidentiality agreement, had responded to their questions with vague and evasive answers. They sometimes lumped the ESOP Committee together with Champion as self-seeking, greedy opportunists. KPS had dealt with similar situations in the past and hired a publicity firm. Psaros and Sutton met with Frank Powers and Phil Smith of Fingerhut, Smith & Associates to plan a comprehensive publicity campaign that would build support for the proposed collective bargaining agreement.[48]

Sutton, who was finding that KPS was relying more and more heavily on him for negotiating the benefit package and selling it to the union membership, was feeling the pressure: "I mean KPS literally said here's a pot of money, go out and buy benefits. And I had to start, first of all, making contacts on who I could get a pension from, who I could get. medical and dental from, who I could get my group life, spouse life and those kind of things. And by the way, who would I set our 401K account with?" Sutton, normally supremely confident, began to doubt his own ability to handle this responsibility. As Gibson explained, "Those kind of things were real important to the people in the union, your benefits, your retirement, stuff like that," no less than "sacred." Union members saw their lucrative benefit package as the defining characteristic of what it meant to be union. It was the security that their parents and grandparents had fought for and won and that they hoped to pass on to their children. Sutton described his misgivings:

They [KPS] were absolutely confident in my abilities to do it,
more so than I was. . . . I was over my head. I learned a lot, I had
a learning curve that was tremendous, and I'm better prepared
now than I was. But, shit, it scared me to death. I'd come home
sometimes, just absolutely physically drained because I didn't
have a friggin' clue what I was doing, yet I was in it. I was up to
my eyebrows in it. I won't begin to tell you that I set the benefits
up and that I'm an all-knowing and all-seeing expert, because I
was scared to death. I had, literally, two-thousand lives in my
hands, as far as being able to provide for with the security that
they'd had before.[49]

Sutton, Psaros, Powers, and Smith came up with an extensive publicity plan. In addition to workers in Canton, Waynesville, and the
Dairy Paks, it identified several more constituencies, including union
members throughout the state and region, union leaders, management, the public and media, and Champion's current customers. It
recommended that the ESOP Committee begin with a telephone poll
to get a clear picture of what the employees were thinking and what
themes and messages should be used in the campaign to create a
favorable attitude toward the proposed contract.[50]

Once the messages were identified and developed, the plan recommended a variety of methods to broadcast them. Some mailings
should be sent to union and management; however, others should be
directed at management alone, for while they wouldn't have a vote
on the contract, their opinions would carry a lot of weight. In addition to the initial announcement letter to employees, which had
already been through six drafts, it suggested publishing a news-sized
tabloid, a summary of the collective bargaining agreement, and a letter from local union leaders and the ESOP Committee, with the last
two going to union members only.[51] The publicity plan also called for
leaflets and handouts for distribution at informational meetings,
posters, stickers, and buttons. It stressed the importance of educating
shop stewards and other union leaders about the issues, so that they
could "be not just supportive, but involved in getting the message out"
and could "be the front-line defense against the rumor mill" that had
already started. The plan also suggested keeping the media informed,

a lesson that the ESOP Committee had already learned, and it stressed the importance of maintaining contact with customers.

Sutton had stressed the need to share as much information as possible with as much of the union membership as possible. He now had serious doubts that the members would approve the contract. His close contacts with the Dairy Paks had led him to think that their votes might doom the effort: "I sure didn't [think the buyout would be approved]. I knew that we wouldn't get any votes in Athens. I was afraid that we probably wouldn't get any in Morristown, but we didn't have a lot of communication with Morristown because it was a UAW. . . . They just made one meeting, so they was pretty unknown. KPS kept telling us that things were going well there, but we didn't have a clue."[52]

The ESOP Committee would have to win over the union membership within two or three months, the expected timeline for finalizing the deal and writing the proposed contract. This made the letter to the employees of critical importance. After seven drafts, it was finally mailed out, in mid-December, and was carefully crafted to convince the membership that this was their single best, if not their only, opportunity to save their jobs. At the same time, it promised a new day of complete openness and sharing of information.[53]

People in the streets, shops and restaurants of Canton were even more in the dark than those inside the plant. Some still refused to believe that Champion would ever sell the mills. Still others, like Ray Warren, had grown tired of the whole issue and attempted to downplay the mill's significance. Warren had worked at Champion in the early 1960s but had left to open a barber shop in downtown Canton. If the mill reduced production or shut down, "Canton won't die," he told a reporter. "The town will survive, but it would hurt." Others, like Skeeter Curtis, owner of Skeeter Barbecue, believed that people would somehow make adjustments and find a way to survive. "It could be really devastating for the town," he said, "but people have to go on. . . . I don't think people are bitter. There was shock at first, then uncertainty, but now we're in a mode of just go on." Some Canton residents, such as Wilber Davis, who owned three businesses in town, had even begun to doubt whether the mill's closing would have much impact at all. "I really don't think it'll have much impact on the town. Many of the workers don't even live here anymore."[54] This sentiment was echoed in a letter to the editor published in the *Enterprise Mountaineer.* Charles Davis suggested that Haywood residents should simply "let Champion leave Haywood County." The following week, Louise Bennett fired back an angry response, saying, "maybe the better idea is to let Mr. Davis leave Haywood County. I don't think that would affect nearly as many lives!" Her response was probably more representative of the majority of citizens. "Everyone, from the real estate salesperson down to the Maytag repairman would be affected," she wrote. "There would be a lot of relocating, which would affect the school system, not to mention the Haywood County tax offices. There's a lot of town and county taxes paid by the employees and Champion as well."

Bennett's comments were also more accurate than those who were suggesting that the mills were not really that important to the town. As Gibson had pointed out, the economic life of the mills was intimately connected to the economic life of the town; the doubters were simply whistling in the dark. In fact, the mill's impact was so broad that it would affect the economic life of the entire county, an argument that Gibson had already used to help convince state government officials to support the buyout.

The ESOP Committee was on unfamiliar ground with the new contract. It would have to go beyond traditional bread-and-butter issues like pay scale and benefits, to include workplace culture issues. The lines between "sides" were blurred; it was no longer enough to just show up with a laundry list of demands for your side and grudgingly give up specific ones in order to reach a compromise. As owners, they were obligated to be sure that the company would remain competitive in the marketplace. This meant trimming nonessentials, becoming "lean and mean," as KPS frequently put it. As unionists they were obligated to see that this was done in the best interests of the workers, guaranteeing them job security, a decent standard of living, and fairness and safety on the job site.

ESOP Committee members, working to finalize the deal with KPS and Champion while at the same time writing a collective bargaining agreement, seemed to be in one long meeting, broken up only occasionally for hastily gobbled meals or a few hours of sleep. Gibson described the frantic pace:

It was real hard because you might find out today that somebody
is in town that you need to meet with for an hour or so. And you
make a call and you say, "I'd like to get with you for a little bit."
"Well, how about let's go out for supper this afternoon, I'll have
a little time off to eat supper." "Sure, we'll go eat." And you run
home and say, I've got to get my clothes changed, I got to go meet
so and so, we're going to eat, we're going to have a meeting and
eat supper and then I'll be back home. It may be two hours later.
We had meetings with our business partners, and it may last till
12, 1 or 2 o'clock in the morning. And you come dragging in at
2 o'clock in the morning and your wife says, "Where in the world
have you been?" "Well, we had a meeting." "This late?" "Well, we
just got through." "Well, what time you got to go in tomorrow?"
"I got to be down there at 7 o'clock in the morning." You get in
bed, three or four hours sleep, it's just like work. The next morning you come in and you start again, 7 o'clock. And you have
meetings maybe that day. And that's what we went through. And
it was rough on everyone.[55]

As the buyout effort approached the final weeks, the pace became
dizzying.

If you took a day-by-day account of everything that went on, it
would be unreal. It really would. Because there was many a time
we'd have a phone in there going, a phone in here talking to
someone else. We'd have someone in here we were talking with,
meeting with, and we'd be scattered that much. And then you
come in here [and meet], "Well, what did he say? What did he
say?" You'd get everybody back up to speed on it. . . . "Well, what
did he say?" It was just a sharing of the knowledge.[56]

Families struggled to support ESOP Committee members. Gibson
credits his wife with holding his family together. While he spent "three
or four" of his vacations in meetings, his wife took his children on real
vacations: "We had stuff going that we just couldn't get away. We tried
to get [committee members] away from here. And we did, we had to
get away sometimes. But then there was times that we couldn't. We
just had to be here, stuff was going on so quick that you needed to
know what was there, so you just had to spend it here. And we've had
to do that, so, you know, it was a hard row to hoe."[57] Haney had always

Kenny Sutton speaks with a KPS attorney by phone as Alton Higgins, Doug Gibson, and Harold Huffman, a union leader from Statesville, North Carolina, work out details of the employee benefit package. As ESOP Committee members attempted to balance jobs, union duties, and finalization of the buyout, they sometimes worked up to twenty hours straight. *Photograph by Debbie Chase-Jennings.* © *1999*, Asheville (N.C.) Citizen-Times. *Reprinted with permission.*

felt the pressure of responsibility during contract negotiations. "I've always been an officer [in the union], because I like dealing with people and I like to try to help if I can," he said. "In negotiations you'll have some people on your side and some against."[58] During one contract negotiation, a few people were very angry over what seemed to Haney to be a minor point. "I don't even remember what it was." Haney commented to a representative from the international, "I don't know why they're so upset."

> And he said . . . the thing that I was talking about wasn't a great big deal to me . . . "but, Richard, you think about it, everything that you do affects somebody's life." I said, "You gotta be kidding."

He says, "No, you think about it. If you give them a raise, if you cause them to lose money, if you change their job, everything that you make a decision on affects their life." And I've thought a lot about that in this ESOP thing. That everything that we were doing wasn't just affecting our lives, but it was affecting over four thousand people. I mean two thousand plus their families. So I figured four or five thousand people, we, as six individuals, are really affecting their lives. Good, bad, or indifferent, we were affecting their lives. And that got me shook a little bit. . . . And you're always trying to affect people's lives for the better, but then when you get to thinking, well, [what if] I messed their lives up forever? . . . it's a little much.[59]

One day, shortly before the contract negotiations between KPS and the union were set to begin in Nashville, Tennessee, the pressure nearly destroyed Haney. At the request of a supervisor, he had been "working graveyard" (overnight shift) in the plant and meeting during the daylight hours.

My boss had called and said they were covered up and they didn't have nobody to fill in. So I said, "Well, I'll work and then come over here the next day to the meeting." I done that a time or two, and when I got off from work I felt good. But by the time I got home my face got to hurting. . . . So I took a couple of pain pills and that didn't help. I was going to sleep a couple of hours and come on down here. And that didn't help and then I took two or three aspirin and they say that's what helped me. But I finally went to sleep and then come on down here and they got on to me about it, and I said, "Well, I had an ear infection." And I really thought it was something to do with my ear because my whole jaw was hurting. The next morning I got up and my whole arm was hurting, . . . and I mentioned it to Kenny and Alton. Well, they didn't say anything then. And then about lunchtime, they called me in here. Kenny said, "You've got three choices." And I said, "What are you talking about?" He said, "You can either go to the doctor, we'll take you to the doctor, or we're going to whip the hell out of you and they can take you in an ambulance." So I said, "Well, I'll go check it out." So I drove up there [to the hospital], and I didn't really think a thing about them coming. But when I looked around and I was in the emergency room and there was Kenny and there was Hutch; they followed me up there.

They said I'd had a heart attack; I still believed it was indigestion. So I stayed overnight, and they run tests and about three weeks later done a heart catheter and said, "Yeah, they needed to do four bypasses." . . . So I was just out about a week. I figured, well hell, I can sit down here just as easy as I can sit down at the house, you know, and I'll at least know what's going on. So they made a big deal about me coming back within a week. But it wasn't I was that great a soldier, it was just that I wanted to be down here instead of at the house by myself. . . . But I've always thrived on stress, I always do my best work under stress. I don't know why, I just, you know, it just seems like when nothing is going on I'm having a bad day.[60]

In mid-February, a letter went out to employees, announcing that a tentative agreement had been reached between the committee and KPS. It was published in the *Enterprise Mountaineer* on February 17. The letter noted that the definitive financial arrangements had to be completed and that the union contract still had to be negotiated, and it reminded the workers that their vote on this contract would constitute the final say in the matter.[61]

Everyone already knew, from press accounts, that the contract would call for a large pay cut and no raises for the seven-year life of the contract. The committee had decided to present the pay reduction as an "investment" in the new company. They would constantly remind union members that if the company made money they could expect to receive even more than the 15 percent in earnings.

Champion officials remained tightlipped. "We are still negotiating," an official said. "It would be incorrect to say that the mills have been sold." Most residents of Haywood County, however, were hopeful and somewhat relieved. Canton restaurateur Skeeter Curtis told a reporter, "Hopefully now the jitters all these employees have been going through will be over." Marvelene Chapman, daughter of a forty-year Champion veteran, expressed the relief that many were feeling. "I would like to see it settled so the people in our town could settle down, be confident in their jobs and go on with their lives."[62]

Charlotte Lackey of the North Carolina Sierra Club was on hand for the press conference announcing the tentative agreement. Her prepared comments were a testament to another of the ESOP Committee's successes, the open, constructive relationship they had built with the environmental community. After describing the impending deal as a "win-win situation," Lackey reiterated one of the principal tenants of worker-ownership: "They'll be much more motivated to take care of their river and air because it's their children who will live there."[63]

As soon as the media lights faded on the celebratory news conference, it was clear that a difficult struggle lay ahead. In a February 18 *Asheville Citizen-Times* article, many employees were carefully noncommittal while others were staunchly opposed to the buyout. "What about five years from now, then what happens?" asked Joanna Howell, a mill employee from Canton.[64] Howell was concerned about the impending wage cuts and about the new company's viability. Ed Moody's comments illustrated the biggest challenge that the Committee faced. "I'm against it. I don't trust the company or the union, either," he said.[65] The issue of trust extended back to Champion's earliest days in Canton. In the early twentieth century, the workers had been promised a job in the Champion family, with the kind of unconditional support that a healthy biological family provides. Instead, in less than twenty years, they had to organize and carry out a determined strike to win a measure of job security. When Reuben Robertson retired, they were promised that nothing would change; the Champion family would continue as it always had. Instead, they found themselves ruled by a board of directors in a far-off northeastern state that showed little understanding of their way of life. And, more recently, they had been offered a chance at cooperative negotiation of a labor contract that would give them a voice in their work rules and interpretation of the contract. Instead, they found themselves under the thumb of a rigid management structure whose interpretation of their cooperative contract was as often as not "my way or the highway."

The workers in Canton and Waynesville carried this collective memory through late 1997 and 1998, while their livelihoods were put on the market and six men met to negotiate deals that would determine their fate. The six were bound by a confidentiality agreement, too nebulous a concept for people who were demanding that the committee "just tell the truth." It was all too secretive, too reminiscent of "business as usual" under Champion. Beneath Ed Moody's complaint that he didn't "trust the union or the company, either," was the memory of a string of betrayals that had made the Champion family a dysfunctional one. Even some comments of those who intended to vote for the buyout contract carried seeds of discontent. Harold Hannah told the *Citizen-Times* that he would vote for the agreement because "it's the only thing we have right now. We're between a rock and hard place." It was a theme that members of the ESOP Committee had resorted to more and more often as the pressures of finalizing the deal and getting approval of the contract mounted.[66]

While the earlier publicity campaigns had stressed the skills of the Champion workforce and how the entire operation would be enhanced by better utilizing the experience and knowledge of the workers, there was now a note of desperation in the committee's public comments. When Higgins asked a *Citizen-Times* reporter "What other alternative do the employees have? . . . wait and see what happens?" he may have pushed some fence-sitters to commit to approving the proposal.[67] But at the same time, these "yes" votes represented lukewarm support. The choice was beginning to sound more like resignation to the inevitable than an exciting opportunity to create a new kind of company.

In early March, informational meetings with the union membership were held at the Canton Middle School auditorium and at each of the Dairy Paks. The ESOP Committee, finally free of the confidentiality constraints that had muzzled it for a year and a half, knew that this series of meetings was critical. The deal would die without employee approval, and beyond this the new company would have little chance to evolve into a more democratically run business without strong support from the employees. Still, a year and a half of intense meetings with investment bankers, government officials, community leaders, independent funding agencies, reporters, and environmentalists had taken a toll. ESOP Committee members were exhausted and found their patience and tolerance stretched at times as they explained matters to their fellow workers. "There was just meeting after meeting after meeting," said Higgins.[68]

One question that was weighing heavily on the minds of every Champion worker over the age of fifty-five with ten years of service came up during the information sessions. What would the retirement pension look like under Blue Ridge Papers? Under Champion, the 55/10 club, as they were known, were awarded two years of service for every year actually worked beyond ten toward their pension. At the time the question was raised, Sutton was negotiating with providers to put together a comprehensive medical and pension benefit package, and he and Higgins responded that the benefit package would have to be different because it would come from a different provider. However, they reiterated their commitment to offering a package that was "as good as or better than" the benefit package they had under Champion.[69]

Later, when the termination agreement that Champion and the union signed stated that Champion would retain responsibility for all those employees who were fifty-five with ten years of service at the time of the sale, Higgins, Sutton, and the rest of the committee believed they had honored their commitment. But the agreement contained some legal vagaries that slipped past the committee and Local 507's attorney. While Champion was legally bound to provide for the 55/10 club, the termination agreement ended the dates of service to the company at the date of the sale. Since these employees would no longer technically be "in service" after this date, the company was only bound to award one year of service for each year over ten instead of the two they would have to offer if the employees had still been in service. Higgins readily acknowledged the oversight, attributing it to "our ignorance." He also expressed regret over the fact that no one correctly interpreted the legalese so that the problem could be fixed before the termination agreement was signed. "We had the opportunity to bridge that but didn't know to," he said. Many rank-and-file union members have been unforgiving, and a vocal minority have accused Sutton and Higgins of deliberately misleading them. "People said, 'Kenny and Alton told us we would retain our same pension plan,'" Higgins said.[70]

Some Canton and Waynesville workers doubted that the ESOP Committee was even now sharing all of the information that it had. "They keep saying they're sworn to secrecy, they're sworn to secrecy . . . , you just can't trust them," said Danny Kirkpatrick. Ed Moody told the *Asheville Citizen-Times* that if the vote were held that day, it would likely fail.[71] Since votes would be tallied together, with each worker at Canton, Waynesville, and all of the Dairy Paks getting one equal vote, the question seemed to come down to how strong support was in the Dairy Paks, which were still a big unknown.

By mid-March there was evidence in employee comments to the press that the informational meetings were having an effect. Tony McCracken commented that he was "still leery" but allowed that the information he had received "does give you something to think about." McCracken also suggested that he and others had begun to see the vote as a choice between the "lesser evil" of a 15 percent wage reduction and no raise for seven years and a "greater evil" of the Canton and Waynesville mills closed, downsized, or owned by a nameless, faceless international mega-corporation that could declare the union and its bargaining agreement null and void. "It's the not knowing that everybody's afraid of," he said, adding that he was "up in the air" about how he would vote. David Sorrells echoed the note of desperation and the sense that the ESOP option was simply the best among a pool of unfavorable options. "I've got a family to feed," he said. "They all need jobs. [Reactions to the buyout option were] a lot more negative to start with, but people are now looking more seriously at it." There were those, such as Harold Messer, who had been won over and were enthusiastically supporting the buyout. "I'm all for it," he said. Messer saw the 15 percent reduction in his paycheck as "an investment in keeping their jobs and an investment in stock."[72]

On Monday, March 29, the ESOP Committee reached another milestone when it finalized a definitive agreement with KPS and Champion over the terms of the buyout. But even this momentous achievement, which had seemed doubtful only a year before, came with a shadow. Someone at KPS expressed reservations about naming a company that specialized in liquid packaging "Sunburst." He noted that one of the biggest concerns in the primary market for paper containers, drink producers, was that paper wasn't strong enough to survive shipping. In fact, this concern was why many were turning to glass and plastic, leading some to believe that paper liquid packaging would someday be obsolete. For this reason, the KPS representative felt that customers would have an initial negative reaction to a company with "burst" in its name.[73]

Up until this time, KPS had managed to avoid one mistake that others involved in the buyout had made: making decisions on behalf of the ESOP Committee without first consulting them. In fact, their care to consult the committee about all substantial matters and to remain available for consultation was one of the things about KPS that impressed the committee most. On this occasion, however, Psaros and Shapiro may have been feeling the pressure to move ahead with the deal, or they may have underestimated the historical and political significance of the name Sunburst. Sutton believed that Gordon Jones, who would eventually be named the new CEO, did not like the name and had convinced others that it should be changed. Whoever made the decision, Champion's March 29 press release announcing that a deal had been reached referred to the new ESOP company as the "Carolina Paper Company."[74]

The ESOP Committee, knowing nothing of this decision that had been made in New York, continued to refer to the company as Sunburst Papers, which resulted in the *Asheville Citizen-Times* calling the company Sunburst while the national press was calling it Carolina Papers. The fact that KPS made the change without consulting the ESOP Committee is what rankled them most. It smacked of the old days under Champion, the "flavor of the month" approach to marketing and production decisions where high-level management made far-reaching changes without consulting the workforce in Canton. Often, these decisions had proved to be ill-planned in ways that could have been avoided if they had first consulted the workers. Sutton, who was both attached to the name Sunburst and to the idea that decisions would be made differently in the new company, read of the name change in the newspaper shortly before Shapiro and Psaros arrived in Canton to appear at a press conference. He was livid. He met Shapiro in the parking lot at Local 507 and an argument ensued. In frustration, Sutton turned and stormed away, then paused and hurled his nearly full soft drink can in Shapiro's direction, where it came to rest at Shapiro's feet.[75]

Inside the union hall, the other ESOP Committee members were milling about in tan T-shirts with the prominent Sunburst logo stitched over the left breast. They had donned the shirts specifically for the press conference, and when they heard the news of the name change, they solemnly retreated to a back room to change.[76] By the time the press conference began, Sutton and Shapiro had mustered enough professionalism to stand together with Higgins on the stage in a show of unity. Psaros was careful to refer to Carolina Paper Company as "the legal entity formed to purchase the Canton system," and he explained that the actual name would be chosen shortly.[77] Sutton and the other committee members finally decided that "if you look at what could have happened, the name is just the name."[78] But still, they had given KPS a forceful reminder that they had struggled mightily during the past eighteen months to free themselves from the domination of a distant corporate office and had no intention of going back.

At the press conference, Higgins expressed relief and marveled at how far he and the committee had come. "There's been a lot of anxiety and frustration," he said. "When this all started, I didn't know how to spell fiduciary responsibility; now I'm right in the middle of it."[79]

All of the constituencies they had courted support from were represented. Governor Hunt released a statement praising the committee's work. "The people of Haywood County and Western North Carolina will benefit tremendously from the employee buyout," it said. "The transition team has worked tirelessly with local and state partners to make this plan a reality and to offer a second chance for the region's economy." Speaking through a conference call hookup, North Carolina's secretary of commerce, Rick Carlisle, was effusive. "This represents one of the most important buyouts in the country," he said. Local government officials, such as C. W. Hardin, mayor of Canton, and Jim Stevens, chair of Haywood County's board of directors, were equally complimentary. "What's $100,000 when it can keep 1,100 jobs here?" asked Stevens, in a reference to the controversial donation the board had made over a year before.[80] Pat Brinkley, representing the Rural Economic Development Center and Western North Carolina Development Association, claimed that the buyout "could mean a lot to the economy of Western North Carolina, but also to other areas," by what it had "inspired others to do."[81]

One of the most impressive, and still most unlikely, shows of support came from Bob Seay of the Dead Pigeon River Council (DPRC). This same organization that had battled Champion International in the courts, in the media, and in sometimes rowdy street demonstrations "congratulate[d] the mill workers on their acquisition of the former Champion facility." Seay was careful to lay the responsibility for the Pigeon River's polluted state with Champion, the corporate entity, and not with the workers, a distinction that squared with the new com-

Kenny Sutton and David Shapiro, the *S* in KPS, look on at the press conference as Alton Higgins makes the official announcement. Champion, KPS, and the ESOP Committee (known as the "Sunburst Transition Team") have reached an agreement. It's now up to the union membership to accept or reject it. *Photograph by Debbie Chase-Jennings. © 1999, Asheville (N.C.) Citizen-Times. Reprinted with permission.*

pany's tactics for dealing with anticipated legal challenges on environmental issues. The DPRC was "gratified that those workers will be in a position to determine their own destiny," and it "call[ed] upon the workers to join them in holding Champion International responsible for the cleanup of 40 feet of toxic sludge containing dioxin, mercury, cyanide and other harmful substances that have been deposited by Champion in Waterville Lake."[82]

The endorsement that had been the longest in coming, and that was necessary for the buyout to be anything more than a pipe dream, came at last. Champion's CEO, Richard Olson, finally broke the company's long silence. "We are pleased to have reached an agreement to sell these facilities," he said. "Our employees at these facilities have served Champion well in the past and now will have a new and exciting future as part of the new company."[83] In a press release, Adams was quick to frame the buyout in broader social terms and

SACCO's vision for social change. SACCO's "involvement in the employee buy-out process that culminated in today's announcement revolves around our commitment to democracy in the workplace," he wrote. Chris Just, who was at the press conference, expressed hope that SACCO could stay involved with the new company, helping to foster a genuinely democratic workplace. "We want to offer workshops to educate employees on how employee stock ownership works and to empower the employees to continue fighting that fight," he said.[84]

Adams and Just knew that the struggle for workplace democracy had hardly begun. For while the workers would own close to half of the company's stock, KPS, with corporate offices far away in New York City, would still own a majority. Unless the workers continued to "fight that fight," as Just had said, the new company risked falling under the sway of the same bureaucratic, top-down management style that had characterized the Champion years. Specifically, the deal called for 55 percent of the stock to go to KPS and a co-investor named General Electric Capital. Collectively, the workers would control 40 percent of the stock through a stock-ownership plan account, and the remaining 5 percent would be offered to senior management. While the employees were stockholders and could vote at annual shareholder meetings, and while they had significant representation on the board of directors, they were clearly minority partners in both roles.

The press conference also confirmed what employees had learned through the press and the shop-floor grapevine; the workers would be asked to take a 15 percent cut in some combination of wages and benefits and to work with no raise in salary for seven years. Sutton was quick to point out they preferred "to consider the cuts as an investment, not a concession."[85] He went on to explain that the shares the workers would receive in return for wages could translate into dollars in-hand if the company were profitable.

The following day, April 1, KPS announced that "the company created for the transaction, Carolina Paper Company," had named its chief executive officer. The ESOP Committee had not put Gordon Jones through a formal interview, as they had Terry Brubaker, but Higgins found him to be "a very personable man [who] is very focused on employee ownership. . . . He is someone who comes with high recommendations and who shares our enthusiasm and goals."[86]

Jones had been vice-president and executive officer of Smurfit-Stone Container Corporation, where he was responsible for sales and marketing of the company's paper and pulp business and oversaw the logistical activities of the company. As Carolina Paper would need an aggressive marketing program to retain customers from the Champion era and build a stronger customer base in specialty papers, where it hoped to expand, Jones seemed to have the ideal background. His experience with managing the technical aspects of paper production and his apparent enthusiasm for an employee ownership model were also in his favor. "I am very excited to be involved in such a terrific project," he said in KPS's press release. "The partnership of capital and labor that created this company is unique in the pulp and paper industry, and I am confident that we will prove to be very successful."[87]

Jones waited just a week before touring the Canton and Waynesville mills to meet the workers in person, a move that must have reminded the elder employees of Reuben Robertson's strolls through the plant to check on the welfare of his workers. He even returned later in the evening to be sure he had the opportunity to meet with the graveyard shift. Jones exuded a spirit of openness and inclusiveness when he talked about the upcoming contract vote. "I feel there will be a great confidence if employees get all the information they need to feel comfortable about the buyout so they can make an informed choice."[88]

On the same day that Jones was announced as the new CEO, April 29 was set as the date for the contract vote, the final hurdle that would complete the buyout.[89] With just a little over three weeks left, the committee poured all of its energy into the informational meetings. Sutton would play a central role in this round of meetings. "I got the short straw, 'cause I could stand in front of people, and I could talk about benefits, and I was actually the person getting the benefits together," he said. Sutton was assigned to accompany Bob Smith, vice-president of the international, to the informational sessions at the Dairy Paks. Sutton noticed right off that, as much as the Haywood County workers might complain about a 15 percent pay reduction, it was the workers in the Dairy Paks who would feel the economic pinch the worst and who would be the hardest sell.

> I had one lady to say, "Look, you don't even have a damn clue what I'm telling you." She said, "you bunch of hillbillies in North

Carolina, up there making nineteen to twenty dollars an hour, I'm making twelve and thirteen dollars an hour." She said, "I can afford to take 15 percent of nineteen or twenty dollars an hour." I said, "Ma'am, we set our living standards toward what we're making. Nineteen and twenty dollars an hour—those people are no better off than the people who are making twelve and thirteen dollars an hour, 'cause they set their living standards accordingly." "You're taking money out of my kids' mouths. You're taking grocery money. You're taking trailer payments. You're taking truck payments." And we were. We were asking for that. . . . She looked at me with big tears in her eyes. Calling me every son-of-a-bitch you could call me and [said] for me to get my ass back across the mountain and leave her alone.[90]

Such confrontations with "people that you've fought so hard for, for years," filled Sutton with doubts.

In the end, Sutton was "terribly proud" and believed that the ESOP Committee had "fought for the interests of everybody. . . . We could have put profit-sharing in, applied toward a percentage of your wages, which we didn't. . . . The guy at Olmstead Falls [is] giving about five thousand to six thousand dollars to this venture yearly, where we're giving ten to twelve. We're getting the same amount of profit-sharing, spread equally across the board. . . . We felt like that was the right thing to do."[91]

On April 29, the polls at Local 507's union hall were open at 5:30 a.m. Over the course of the day, nearly 80 percent of the eligible voters in Haywood County stopped by to cast their ballot. The ballot count in Canton and Waynesville continued until early the next morning. Throughout the night, the ESOP Committee, KPS representatives, and supporters waited expectantly at a local hotel to celebrate. A catered buffet stood off to the side, hardly touched by committee members, who spent much of the evening on the phone with reporters.[92]

The final word came in time to make the early edition of the *Asheville Citizen-Times.* Its inch-tall bold headlines read "Champion buyout approved." Local 507 had voted 606–420 in favor, but the most important figure was a systemwide 927–600 approval count. All of the Dairy Paks had approved the deal, save Athens, Georgia, which rejected it 113–4.[93] According to Sutton, Athens workers believed that

they could make it as a stand-alone facility because of their offset press
that produced the graphics on juice cartons:

> Athens kept thinking that their facility, although we would prob-
> ably die, and some of the other facilities would die, that they
> would go on, and that somebody would scarf them up, because
> of that new offset press that they had. And that they could con-
> tinue to make the wages that they're making without having to
> make any investments. That's what they were being told. And it
> was kindly like, "the hell with you." You know, "we're gonna sur-
> vive out of this, but it's, at this point, every man for himself. If
> Canton dies, or Olmstead Falls dies, or Morristown dies, that's
> fine, but we're gonna live through this, because we've got the off-
> set press."[94]

A name search revealed that International Papers Inc. held a pro-
prietary interest in the name "Carolina Papers," so KPS executives,
this time with input from the ESOP Committee, came up with yet
another name. They chose Blue Ridge Paper Products, and the new
name was announced in the press accounts of the contract approval.

According to Corey Rosen, executive director of the National
Center for Employee Ownership in Oakland, California, the worker-
owners of Blue Ridge Paper Products had pulled off one of the ten
largest employee buy-outs in American history and the largest ever in
the Southeast. It was the first employee buyout on record in the U.S.
forest manufacturing industry.[95]

In the aftermath of the vote, Local 507's president James Hutchinson
remembered the nearly overwhelming challenges that each member
of the ESOP Committee had faced during the eighteen-month effort.
"The committee assumed a lot of responsibility," he said. "I've spent a
lot of time traveling back and forth to Duke Hospital with my twenty-
three-year-old daughter Cindy, who was diagnosed with [lymphoma]."
Hutchinson remembered Richard Haney's heart attack, suffered during an ESOP Committee meeting, his subsequent bypass surgery, and
his speedy return to both his job in the mill and his duties on the committee.[96] Higgins, the committee's chair, had begun his tenure by going
through a divorce and ended it consoling family members over a death
and making funeral arrangements even while the final union contract

was being negotiated. Daniel Gregg had supported his wife through a serious illness, and Doug Gibson had limped along, postponing treatment for a knee injury that would eventually require reconstructive surgery.[97] Through it all, these men had honored their commitments to family, their jobs, and their union. Ultimately, they fought for the very survival of their community, all the while bearing criticism and verbal assaults from coworkers who suspected they were taking advantage of the situation to line their own pockets.

Committee members express few regrets or second thoughts. They simply chose to do the "right thing" and determined never to waver until it was accomplished. Haney, with a penchant for framing things in a larger perspective, put it well. He was motivated by "something, deep inside that I feel was the right thing to do. And if it all falls through tomorrow, I won't have any real regret over it. Because I think it's something that needed to be done. I really believe that somewhere out there in the future, that if we set an example that you'll see it [employee ownership] happening all over the place." Or, as Higgins said, "we took it upon ourselves that if we do the right thing, and we tell our story it will be heard. And it was. It really was. And that's the great part of this. That it was accepted and it was heard." And when Sutton was asked if knowing what he knows now he would do it again, he didn't hesitate. "Yes. Yeah, it was the right thing to do. It was the right thing to do."[98]

Perhaps the most remarkable thing about this story is that Henson, Haney, Gibson, Sutton, Higgins, and Gregg had nothing in their background that might suggest that they would one day carry out something as extraordinary as leading one of the largest employee buyouts in U.S. history. They were factory workers with no special training and little formal education. Yet they chose to persevere and, against all odds, accomplished a heroic feat.

Epilogue

Four years after the employees of the Canton system became part owners of Blue Ridge Paper Products, Alton Higgins sat in Local 507's
union hall thinking about the experience. He was considering the
question of whether or not the new company, with 40 percent
employee ownership, had created any real changes on the shop floor.
Had the workplace at Blue Ridge become more democratic? Was the
vast store of knowledge and experience that the workers had accu-
mulated being tapped? Or was the main office, now located locally,
still operating in the same autocratic top-down power structure.

"The biggest failure I see," he said, "is that we failed to structure
it in a way that would take it down to the floor immediately for people
on the floor to be involved from the get-go. That would be the thing
I would change." Higgins could still imagine a company where all
employees "would be involved in every step, every angle, every department in the company." He would like to see the traditional top-down
hierarchy replaced with a series of concentric circles, with each area
of the plant represented by a workplace culture committee and area
culture committees represented by department workplace culture
committees. Department committees would send representatives to
a company steering committee "that would address just global, major
issues. . . . Departments would work on their own safety issues, education, training, employee involvement, everything having to do with
their own department."[1]

Higgins's vision suggests that a change in control of capital might
provide an opportunity for a change in power relations in the workplace and might even lead to greater democracy in the workplace.
However, such systemic changes have proved to be Blue Ridge's
biggest challenge, because, as Adams has said, "in effect, discussing
worker ownership and the application of democracy upsets traditional
power relationships, both externally and internally."[2] In December of
2002, historian Gar Alperovitz spoke about the worker ownership and

ESOP movements and suggested that they were part of a "slow, evolutionary construction of something new" in America's fundamental sociopolitical structure. He noted that "political systems are defined by who owns the property and the capital" and that they "come and go, historically, they don't last forever." Alperovitz then turned to the prospect of creating a state that was "neither capitalist nor socialist."[3]

Alperovitz sees worker ownership as a "moral spearhead" at a time when "democracy is a declining belief." The extreme concentrations of wealth among fewer and fewer people and a legal system that seems more concerned with the rights of corporate entities than individuals has created an apathetic populace that feels our core values of democracy, equality, and liberty are being routinely violated. These are the "preconditions for what is called a systemic crisis," he said. "It is no longer possible to continue to affirm that this is a workable way to achieve those values." But Alperovitz puts a positive spin on the apathy and cynicism, seeing it as a necessary step as people begin to realize that the current system just isn't working. Worker ownership models, ESOPS, and those who work for them represent a "prerequirement of even imagining what might be the next way forward in the new century."[4]

Significantly for Blue Ridge Papers, Alperovitz sees the role of labor unions as pivotal in the process of extending democracy through dispersing capital throughout the company, but it is not the traditional political role that labor has played. Labor is "a central piece in liberal politics," he said, "but it is a declining force." The social democratic model, with a strong welfare state and unions effectively winning and protecting workers' rights, is a thing of the past. "The power base, labor, has fallen. Organized labor has dropped." Alperovitz noted that many in the labor movement "had a narrow view," but labor has had to reach out and form labor-community alliances because it is weaker. Several unions have begun to advocate for worker-ownership, even sometimes using their sacred pension funds for the effort.[5]

The United Paperworkers International Union (UPIU) provided strong support to Local 507's efforts to buy the Canton system. Adams was well aware of the importance of the international's support and went to great pains from the beginning to win it. But since the buyout was completed, during this critical time that would define the new company's culture, the picture is a bit cloudier. The way Sutton sees it, Local 507 failed to change anything, and rather than leading the way toward a new, more democratic workplace culture, it has reverted to old, rigid patterns of confrontation that threaten to destroy Blue Ridge Paper. "This whole idea of [employee] ownership has not happened and will not happen until people on all sides change the way they think. I think they're doomed unless they realize that they are owners," he said. He fears that Blue Ridge could easily suffer the fate of the Ecusta Mill, another UPIU shop just thirty miles away in Brevard, North Carolina, that had demanded a 12 percent raise. At the time of the interview, the company had shut down production for eight months. "Right or wrong, not judging whether it should have been there or shouldn't have been there, what I'm saying is that sometimes 12 percent or zero is the options you have. And a realistic person is going to try to save enough to fight again another day."[6]

To a man, the ESOP Committee members believe that their greatest success is that they did in fact save enough to fight another day. Until the decision to shut down the Morristown, New Jersey, Dairy Pak in 2003, a decision that was made at the higher levels of management, not a single job had been lost in the Canton system. In fact, Blue Ridge had hired new employees during its first four years of existence in an industry in which forty mills and 104 paper-making machines were closed in 2001–2 alone.

Higgins was quick to point out that the Canton and Waynesville mills could have easily suffered the fate of Champion's Hamilton, Ohio, mill. Early in the buyout process, the ESOP Committee had invited the Hamilton local to join in the buyout effort, but the Ohio workers refused. They later tried to initiate an employee buyout on their own, which failed. The Hamilton mill was subsequently bought by Sun Capital, an investment firm that specializes in buying up struggling companies at bargain rates. "They're going to shut the mill down for a day. And the result is that everybody will be a new hire without benefits, without pension, without seniority, without respect to the union or to the contract. They have said that there'll be anywhere from a 25 percent to a 30 percent reduction in wages. And that the managers had been told to turn in all of their keys, clean out their lockers, everybody has to turn in a new application for employment and will be rehired on that basis." Sutton and Gregg also acknowledged that the buyout had helped the union achieve one of its most important functions, saving jobs.[7]

But all agree that the "whole workplace initiative" has not been "taken down to the floor." And while there is contention as to the cause, most agree that the same top-down hierarchical management process exists in Blue Ridge as it did in Champion. Gregg, in fact, believes that it may be worse. He is troubled by what seems to be a veil of secrecy between salaried management and hourly workers. No one is quite sure what managers earn, but the workers have been told that their manager salaries have been staked to a nationwide norm. Gregg feels this has created a double-standard, since the workers were willing to take a 15 percent cut to save the company. "Workplace culture is a good thing," he said, "but if all the players are not on the same level of understanding, and we're not all rolling together, I don't think it would, no matter what the circumstances, work out for the betterment of the company."[8]

This, along with the fact that Blue Ridge has hired managers at a higher rate than even Champion did, creating what Gregg refers to as "unnecessary layers of management," has created a tense and contentious atmosphere in the mills. Immediately after the buyout, according to Gregg, there was a honeymoon period of goodwill and positive optimism between management and labor. "Things were communicated, things were understood," in regard to the contract. Outstanding grievances were settled, and it looked as though a more cooperative workplace culture was indeed emerging, characterized by "a good, steady understanding of everything, both from the union perspective and management." But Gregg believes that someone at the corporate level "took a stand to say we're not going to give this [communication and cooperation] priority."[9]

The result sounds hauntingly like the Canton system of the early 1990s, when the union sat down with the company to negotiate a contract based on common understanding of mutual interests, that allowed for a certain vagueness in the language with the understanding that subsequent disputes would be ironed out through mutually respectful negotiation. At that time, new managers were brought in who insisted on interpreting the letter of the contract and implementing it unilaterally. It was not long before grievances mushroomed.

This time, "the trouble that we had before left and then came back," according to Gregg. One of the early signs of trouble occurred as grievances began piling up and "a certain member of management that worked well with the union was . . . kind of on the chop-block and was fired." His replacement was a manager who Gregg felt had "created a lot of the hostilities," left the company, but then was hired back "at a higher salary."[10]

The fact that Sutton had become a salaried manager during the first year of the company's life also fed the mistrust of the ESOP Committee that had built over the eighteen months that the confidentiality agreement with Champion was in place. Higgins had also "gone salary," though under different circumstances. Shortly after becoming a vice-president of Blue Ridge, George Henson had asked Higgins to take on a unique and critical role. He wanted Higgins to "stay in the union hall" and work as a "consultant for the union and the company." Higgins was asked to play point man in the transition to an employee-owned company. His job would be to work as an educator and as a consultant, to be on the culture team of the Canton system. The new culture of worker-ownership would require a new way of relating between union and management, settling differences quickly and efficiently, in order for the new company to survive. Blue Ridge would not have deep pockets, as Champion had, so any work stoppage or dip in production for resolving grievances or arbitration could have a devastating effect on the company's success.[11]

Henson saw Higgins's role as critical, and Higgins agreed. He was to be the lead educator in nurturing this new culture. But as he said, he would be "in no-man's-land," not quite in the union and not quite in the company. Henson's choice of Higgins was very deliberate. He told Higgins, "You have the vision. You are the one who knows all of the details of this process from the beginning and of how the new company should operate."[12] Higgins knew that he was walking into a mine field. He had been a committed union man his entire working life, serving as steward and later local officer. At the same time, he was possessed of a mind that saw both sides of every issue and a commitment to fairness and equity that went deeper than traditional union/management ideologies. It was these qualities that led Henson to recruit Higgins for the new role.

For a man with this kind of integrity, the pressures of such a high-profile, political role would prove to be almost overwhelming. For two years Higgins went to work at the union hall, helping the rank and file understand their new medical and retirement benefits, dealing with all of the "traditional union issues." Higgins believed that he was "setting the tone for the new Blue Ridge" to become a company operated by worker-owners at every level. Though in a radically different context, he struggled to fill a role that only Reuben Robertson had been successful at, being the primary contact to every aspect of the operation, from the CEO to the hourly worker.[13] But Higgins never had the god-like status of Robertson conferred on him. In union elections held in late 1999, he recalled how "the traditionalists ran on getting me out of the union hall, straightening out all of the wrongs that [the ESOP Committee] had created." Higgins, understandably, found it hard not to take the attacks personally. "It broke my heart," he said. "I could have gone to work as a salaried employee at any point." This would have given him a higher salary, more security, and less stress. "When I decided to work in the union hall [as a consultant] I was taking things away from my family" by remaining an hourly employee and not taking the higher paid salary position. "I could have slept better if I'd picked up my tools and gone back into the mill."[14] Higgins acknowledges that the anger and hurt he felt at being the scapegoat for every problem the union faced and at being accused of lining his own pockets caused him to over-react. When an offer came from Blue Ridge to do the same kind of work he had been trying to do in Canton in the Dairy Paks, to educate union and management about employee empowerment and to nurture a workplace culture characterized by cooperation and open communication, Higgins jumped at the chance.

For those workers who wanted to believe that members of the ESOP Committee were motivated only by self-interest, Sutton and Higgins had confirmed their suspicions. Gregg is quick to say that he has no problem with someone trying to better his position, but he is concerned about how their move affected "the accountability and the integrity" of the ESOP Committee. "I was always reiterating that what we were there for was to do as good a job for all of the people that we represent as for ourselves," he said.[15]

Sutton gives short shrift to complaints that they had somehow betrayed the union constituency. In fact, he claims that the ESOP Committee "allowed Alton and I to lead. They several times insisted on it. We had several conversations during that eighteen months that this is a two-man show." But according to Sutton, when he and Higgins tried to share the responsibilities of leadership, "every time we tried to push it out, it always come back. It was always pushed back to us. I remember saying, 'Well, if they're going to let us lead, we got to lead. . . .' We would take special care in pushing some of this out to these guys," but the responsibilities of leadership "always got pushed back."[16]

Gregg cites further misunderstandings over how the profit-sharing plan would work. He and others claim that they were led to believe that all of the company's profits would be shared with the worker-owners or that they would have a voice in whether or not the profits would be distributed or reinvested. In fact, many had been convinced to give up 15 percent of their compensation for the prospect that they could get it back, and perhaps even more, through profit sharing. But to date there have been only a very few small profit-sharing checks, while much of the profit has been reinvested without their input.[17]

Perhaps Richard Haney is a lodestar for the future of Blue Ridge Paper Products and the employee ownership movement as a whole. He is clearly torn, a man with a life of committed service to the union movement and all it represents—worker rights, job safety and security, and a fair day's pay for a fair day's work. Yet during the eighteen months he led the buyout of Champion, he became a true convert to employee ownership and the idea that workers who owned and controlled their company's capital were more qualified than anyone else to protect these rights. "I feel like, with a true ESOP, that no matter what the [contract] language is, or whether its structured out, that if you've got rational people you can work out any problem that you've got." He does not hide the fact that he has been disappointed. "I anticipated this company being a showplace, really, for the whole country.

And I've got reservations." Still, he has no regrets and remains committed to the ESOP concept and to making Blue Ridge's ESOP work: "Even with having a difference, I believe an ESOP committee or an ESOP company could work it out. And maybe our workplace culture now is going in the right direction. We've got a federal mediator talking with both sides and meeting with them. I think its silly. I'm not opposed to mediation, but I think if everybody was really looking at the right avenue, management and union, that you don't need a mediator."[18]

In a sense, Haney's analysis holds the most promise. He does not deny the hard realities and struggle that lie ahead to win power from a company of which they are now part owners. Neither is he willing to compromise his vision or his faith that Blue Ridge Paper Products can emerge from the struggle as a true democratically operated enterprise. His faith is not blind; it grows from experience, an eighteen-month struggle in which he and five fellow workers refused to buckle under the pressures of an international corporation, the indifferences of a state government, or the skepticism and resistance of their own fellow workers. In the end, they won the respect and support of all of these, and this achievement alone is enough to justify Haney's faith.

Notes

CHAPTER 1

1. Vanise Henson, interview by the author, 27 Oct. 1999.
2. Alton Higgins, interview by the author, 27 Oct. 1999.
3. Daniel Gregg, interview by the author, 17 Nov. 1999.
4. Doug Gibson, interview by the author, 21 Dec. 1999.
5. Richard Haney, interview by the author, 17 Nov. 1999.
6. Tracy Davis, "Canton Mill for Sale," *Asheville Citizen-Times,* 9 Oct. 1997, final ed., A1.
7. Henson, interview.
8. Higgins, interview.
9. Gregg, interview.
10. Haney, interview.
11. Gibson, interview.
12. Kenny Sutton, interview by the author, 2 May 2000.

CHAPTER 2

1. U.S. Bureau of the Census, *Statistical Abstract of the United States, 1997,* 117 ed. (Washington, D.C.: Government Printing Office, 1997), 441.
2. *Western North Carolina Labor History,* on file at the Asheville-Buncombe Main Library, Asheville, N.C. (Hereafter cited as *WNC Labor History.*)
3. Philip S. Foner, *History of the Labor Movement in the United States* (New York: International), 1:518–19.
4. *WNC Labor History.*
5. Lewis L. Lorwin, *The American Federation of Labor* (Washington D.C.: Brockings Institution, 1933), 21; quoted in Foner, *History,* 2:141.
6. Foner, *History,* 2:142.
7. Biltmore Estate Web Page, at http://www.ky.essortment.com/biltmore-housea_rguh.htm. See also "Western NC Attractions: Biltmore Estate," at http://www.westernncattractions.com/biltmore.htm (accessed 14 May 2001).
8. *WNC Labor History.*
9. Ibid.
10. Allen Roudebush, ed., *Memoirs of Reuben Robertson, Sr., Volume II* (Champion International Corp., 1991), sec. 17:1–2.
11. Ibid., sec. 17:2.

12. Reuben B. Robertson, "Keep 'em Human: The Vital Role of Sound Labor Relations in Bringing Victory" (an address presented to the National Association of Manufacturers Wartime Institute on Industrial Relations, French Lick, Ind., Aug. 1942), in Roudebush, *Memoirs of Reuben Robertson,* 8.

13. Champion Fibre Co., *The Champion Guide: A Book of Information and Instruction for "The Champion Family"* (Canton, N.C.: Champion Fibre Co., [1923?]), 7–8.

14. James Hutchinson, interview by the author, 2 Feb. 2001.

15. Haney, interview.

16. Charles Cable, interview by the author, 3 Apr. 2001.

17. Hutchinson, interview.

18. Cable, interview.

19. Ibid.

20. B. H. DePriest, "Welfare Work at Canton," *Carolina Mountaineer,* 21 Dec. 1916, 20, Haywood County Industrial and Resort Edition. Reprint of a Special Industrial and Resort Edition of the *Carolina Mountaineer* sponsored by the Haywood County Historical Society.

21. A. D. Wood, "Canton: The Place to Work: An Interview with Tom, Dick and Harry," *Carolina Mountaineer,* 21 Dec. 1916, 20.

22. Cable, interview.

23. Ibid.

24. Ibid.

25. H. W. Sullivan, "Correspondence from Vice President Sullivan," *Journal: Official Organ of the International Brotherhood of Pulp, Sulphite, and Paper Mill Workers* 7, no. 64 (1917): 8.

26. Haney, interview.

27. Ibid.

28. Roudebush, *Memoirs of Reuben Robertson,* sec. 26:1–3.

29. E. Kaye Lanning, "Champion Fibre Company: Industry in Western North Carolina" (master's thesis, Univ. of North Carolina at Chapel Hill, 1980), 57–58, 60–61.

30. Ibid., 58–59.

31. Henson, interview; Lanning, "Champion Fibre Company," 59.

32. Lanning, "Champion Fibre Company," 59.

33. Cable, interview.

34. Lanning, "Champion Fibre Company," 60.

35. Cable, interview.

36. Lanning, "Champion Fibre Company," 60.

37. Ibid., 61.

38. Cable, interview.

39. Lanning, "Champion Fibre Company," 61.

40. *Asheville Citizen,* 23 Feb. 1924, quoted in Lanning, "Champion Fibre Company," 61.

41 Lanning, "Champion Fibre Company," 63.

42 Henson, interview.

43 Lanning, "Champion Fibre Company," 62, 63–64.

44 Also known as Ella May Wiggins, she dropped the surname of her husband, John Wiggins, after he left her in the mid-1920s. All of her surviving children, save one, did likewise.

45 John A. Salmond, *Gastonia, 1929: The Story of the Loray Mill Strike* (Chapel Hill: Univ. of North Carolina Press, 1995). See also Lynn Haessly, "Mill Mother's Lament: Ella May, Working Women's Militancy, and the 1929 Gaston County Strikes" (master's thesis, Univ. of North Carolina at Chapel Hill, 1987).

46 *Asheville Citizen,* 4 March 1924, quoted in Lanning, "Champion Fibre Company," 63–64.

47 George Stoney and Judith Helfand, *The Uprising of '34,* VHS (First Run/ Icarus Films, 1995).

48 Cable, interview.

49 Joanita M. Nellenbach, "The Birth of Local 507: Organizers Remember Struggle to Unionize Champion's Mill," *Waynesville Mountaineer,* 4 Sept. 1995, A6.

50 Gibson, interview.

51. Quoted in Nellenbach, "The Birth of Local 507," A6.

52 John Scroggs, interview by the author, 3 Apr. 2001.

53 Quoted in Nellenbach, "The Birth of Local 507," A6.

54 Scroggs, interview.

55 Ibid.

56 Ibid.

57. Cable, interview.

58 Office of University Development, Univ. of North Carolina, Chapel Hill, at http://www.dev.unc.edu/development/distprofs/moore.htm (accessed 30 Apr. 2001).

59. Cable, interview.

60. Scroggs, interview.

61. Cable, interview.

62. Ibid.

63. Ibid.

64. Ibid.

65. Nellenbach, "The Birth of Local 507," A6.

66. Cable, interview.

67. Ibid.

68. Ibid.
69. Ibid.
70. Ibid.

CHAPTER 3

1. John Authers, "Champion to Sell Units and Cut Workforce," *Financial Times: World Business Newspaper,* 9 Oct. 1997, 26. Accessed in Factiva, 7 July 2003, at http://global.factiva.com.

2. Higgins, interview, 27 Oct. 1999.

3. Haney, interview.

4. L. J. Rose, "Daily Log: Personal," 24, 27 Oct. 1997. In the possession of L. J. Rose, Covington, VA.

5. Frank Adams, *Unearthing Seeds of Fire: The Idea of Highlander* (Winston-Salem, N.C.: Blair, 1974), introduction.

6. Frank Adams, interview by the author, 8 June 2000.

7. Gibson, interview.

8. Frank Adams to the author, e-mail, 26 July 2001.

9. Ibid.

10. Frank Adams, conversation with the author, 9 June 2000.

11. Adams, e-mail.

12. Rose, "Daily Log," 3, 4 Nov. 1997.

13. Ibid.

14. Haney, interview.

15. Gregg, interview.

16. Higgins, interview, 27 Oct. 1999.

17. Rose, "Daily Log," 4 Nov. 1997.

18. Higgins, interview, 27 Oct. 1999.

19. Haney, interview.

20. Gibson, interview.

21. Haney, interview.

22. Gibson, interview.

23. Higgins, interview, 27 Oct. 1999.

24. Henson, interview.

25. Rose, "Daily Log," 6 Nov. 1997.

26. Higgins, interview, 27 Oct. 1999.

27. Rose, "Daily Log," 6 Nov. 1997.

28. Ibid., 10 Nov. 1997.

29. Gregg, interview.

30. Rose, "Daily Log," 10 Nov. 1997.

31. Ibid.

32. Ibid.

33. Rose, "Daily Log," 13 Nov. 1997; Adams, interview.

34. Rose, "Daily Log," 13 Nov. 1997.

35. Ibid.

36. Adams, interview.

37. Rose, "Daily Log," 13 Nov. 1997.

38. Sutton, interview, 2 May.

39. Rose, "Daily Log," 13 Nov. 1997.

40. Ibid.

41. Higgins, interview, 27 Oct. 1999.

42. Gibson, interview.

43. Gregg, interview.

44. Haney, interview.

45. Henson, interview.

46. Rose, "Daily Log," 13 Nov. 1997.

47. Kenny Sutton, interview by the author, 3 Mar. 2003.

48. Ibid.

CHAPTER 4

1. ESOP Committee minutes, Smoky Mountain Local 507 Union Hall, Canton, N.C., Nov. 18, 1997.

2. Adams, interview.

3. Gregg, interview.

4. Higgins, interview, 27 Oct. 1999.

5. Gibson, interview.

6. Henson, interview.

7. Sutton, interview, 2 May 2000.

8. Ibid.

9. Adams, interview. Daniel Gregg's wife had also been diagnosed with cancer during the course of the buyout effort.

10. "Champion Workers Deserve a Bright and Secure Future," *Asheville Citizen-Times,* 9 Oct. 1997, 6A, editorial.

11. Haney, interview.

12. Sandy Wall and Quintin Ellison, "Canton Mill for Sale," *Asheville Citizen-Times*, 9 Oct. 1997, 1A.

13. ESOP Committee minutes, Smoky Mountain Local 507 Union Hall, Canton, N.C., 18 Nov. 1997.

14. Ibid.

15. Adams, interview.

16. ESOP Committee minutes, Smoky Mountain Local 507 Union Hall, Canton, N.C., 18 Nov. 1997.

17. Ibid.

18. Ibid.

19. Undated press release, ESOP Committee archives, Smoky Mountain Local 507, Canton, N.C.

20. Alton Higgins to James Andrews, 26 Nov. 1997, ESOP Committee archives.

21. Undated letter, ESOP Committee archives.

22. Larry R. Sorrells and Laura Gordon to Alton Higgins, undated, ESOP Committee archives.

23. ESOP Committee minutes, 2 Dec. 1997.

24. Adams, interview.

25. Adams, *Seeds of Fire,* introduction.

26. Larry R. Sorrells to UPIU Local 507, 3 Dec. 1997, ESOP Committee archives.

27. ESOP Committee archives, comments faxed by ACS to Local 507 containing comments for ESOP to use in publicity, 4 Dec. 1997.

28. ESOP Committee minutes, 2 Dec. 1997; Higgins, interview, 27 Oct. 1999.

29. Peggy Gosselin and Vicki Hyatt, "Union Wants to Buy Mill," *Waynesville (N.C.) Enterprise Mountaineer,* 5 Dec. 1997, 1A.

30. Adams, interview.

31. Higgins, interview, 27 Oct. 1999.

32. John Fletcher (photographer), *Asheville Citizen-Times,* ESOP Committee archives.

33. Peggy Gosselin, "Plans for Mill Buyout Released," *Waynesville (N.C.) Enterprise Mountaineer,* 8 Dec. 1997, 1A, 6A.

34. Quinton Ellison, "Workers See Bright Future for Champion," *Asheville Citizen-Times,* ESOP Committee archives.

35. Haney, interview.

36. Roy Kilby to Mike Coleman, 8 Dec. 1997, ESOP Committee archives.

37. David A. Craft to Alton Higgins, 9 Dec. 1997, ESOP Committee archives.

38. Higgins, interview, 27 Oct. 1999.

39. Craft to Higgins, 9 Dec. 1997.

40. James Harrison to Alton Higgins, 14 Dec. 1997, ESOP Committee archives.

41. Mr. and Mrs. F. M. Saunders to "Sir," 11 Dec. 1997, ESOP Committee archives.

42. Gregg, interview.

CHAPTER 5

1. Tracy Davis, "Mill Forced to Cut Back on Discharge," *Asheville Citizen-Times* 12 Dec. 1997, A1.

2. Peggy Gosselin, "Tennessee Groups Drop Appeals," *Waynesville (N.C.) Enterprise Mountaineer,* 24 Dec. 1997, A1.

3. Tracy Davis, "Champion Rules Backed in Tennessee," *Asheville Citizen-Times,* 12 Dec. 1997, ESOP Committee archives.

4. Higgins, interview, 27 Oct. 1999.

5. Richard A. Bartlett, *Troubled Waters: Champion International and the Pigeon River Controversy* (Knoxville: Univ. of Tennessee Press, 1995).

6. Charles "Cromer" Chambers, affidavit furnished Richard A. Bartlett by Dick Mullinix, quoted in Bartlett, *Troubled Waters,* 42.

7. Ibid.

8. Gibson, interview.

9. Henson, interview.

10. Sutton, interview, 2 May 2000.

11. Ibid.

12. Higgins, interview, 27 Oct. 1999.

13. Gregg, interview.

14. Bartlett, *Troubled Waters,* 56–75.

15. Ibid., 139–42

16. Gibson, interview.

17. Gregg, interview.

18. Haney, interview.

19. Bartlett, *Troubled Waters,* 139–52.

20. Gregg, interview.

21. Bartlett, *Troubled Waters,* 141.

22. Ibid., 139–52.

23. Gregg, interview.

24. Ibid.

25. Bartlett, *Troubled Waters,* 150–52.

26. Ibid., 147–52.

27. Ibid., 157–60.

28. Adams, interview.

29. Bartlett, *Troubled Waters,* 160–63.

30. Ibid., 170–78.

31. Gregg, interview.

32. Bartlett, *Troubled Waters,* 174–76.

33. Henson, interview.

34. Sutton, 2 May 2000.

35. Bartlett, *Troubled Waters,* 179–87.

36. Scroggs, 3 Apr. 2001.

37. Bartlett, *Troubled Waters,* 188.

38. Ibid.

39. Haney, interview.

40. Bartlett, *Troubled Waters,* 190–207.

41. Ibid.

42. Ibid.

43. Ibid., 208–17.

44. Ibid., 265–78.

45. Tracy Davis, "Champion Rules Backed in Tennessee, *Asheville Citizen-Times,* 12 Dec. 1997, ESOP Committee archives.

46. Adams, interview.

47. Higgins, interview, 27 Oct. 1999.

48. Sutton, interview, 2 May 2000.

49. Gibson, interview.

50. Gregg, interview.

51. Ginny Lindsey to Alton Higgins, 17 Dec. 1997, ESOP Committee archives.

52. Charlotte E. Lackey to Mike Coleman, 10 Dec. 1997, ESOP Committee archives.

53. Chris Just, interview by the author, 5 Nov. 2003.

54. Adams, interview.

55. Higgins, interview, 27 Oct. 1999.

56. Haney, interview.

57. Henson, interview.

58. Sutton, interview, 2 May 2000.

59. Adams, interview.

60. Ibid.

61. Gibson, interview.

62. Adams, interview.

63. Ibid.

64. J. Philip Neal to Alton Higgins and Kenny Sutton, 24 Dec. 1997, ESOP Committee archives.

65. Adams, interview.

66. Ibid.

67. Higgins, interview, 27 Oct. 1999.

CHAPTER 6

1. "Local Control Could Save Jobs, Help Environment," *Asheville Citizen-Times,* editorial, c. Jan. 1998, ESOP Committee archives.

2. Rose, "Daily Log," 8 Jan. 1998.

3. Gregg, interview.

4. Rose, "Daily Log," 9–15 Jan. 1998.

5. Tracy Davis, "Union Officials Say They Are Closer to Buying Canton Mill," *Asheville Citizen-Times*, 19 Jan. 1998, A1.

6. Haney, interview.

7. Ibid.

8. "Smoky Mountain Local 507 ESOP Research Committee, Request for Commitment-Advantage West," 27 Jan. 1998, ESOP Committee archives.

9. Chris Just, interview by the author, 8 Mar. 2001.

10. Ibid.

11. Ibid.

12. Adams, interview.

13. Rose, "Daily Log," 4–18 Nov. 1997, 5–26 Jan. 1998.

14. Just, interview, 8 Mar. 2001.

15. Higgins, interview, 27 Oct. 1999.

16. Ibid.

17. Ibid.

18. Ibid.

19. Ibid.

20. Ibid.

21. Just, interview, 8 Mar. 2001.

22. Frank Adams to the author, e-mail, 7 July 2003.

23. Rose, "Daily Log," 19 Feb. 1998.

24. Ibid.

25. Ibid., 24 Feb. 1998.

26. Sutton, interview, 2 May 2000.

27. Higgins, interview, 27 Oct. 1999.

28. Gibson, interview.

29. Just, interview, 8 Mar. 2001.

30. Ibid.

31. Rose, "Daily Log," 24 Feb. 1998.

32. Ibid.

33. "Commissioners to Get Update on Union Buyout Plan," *Waynesville (N.C.) Enterprise Mountaineer,* 25 Feb. 1998, ESOP Committee archives.

34. Alton Higgins to Jack Horton, 3 Mar. 1998, ESOP Committee archives.

35. ESOP Committee archives, undated meeting notes.

36. Peggy Gosselin and Vicki Hyatt, "Opinions Mixed Over Grant," *Waynesville (N.C.) Enterprise Mountaineer,* 16 Mar. 1998, A1.

37. Sutton, interview, 2 May 2000.

38. J. A. Cochran, "Champion Gets All the Attention," letter to the editor, *Waynesville (N.C.) Enterprise Mountaineer,* 18 Mar. 1988, ESOP Committee archives.

39. Haney, interview.

40. Sutton, interview, 2 May 2000.

41. Higgins, interview, 27 Oct. 1999.

42. "Commission Gives Champion Purchase a Wise Boost," *Asheville Citizen-Times,* editorial, ESOP Committee archives.

43. Frank Adams to Kenny Sutton, facsimile, 27 Feb. 1998, ESOP Committee archives.

44. Just, interview, 8 Mar. 2001.

45. Ibid.

46. Higgins, interview, 27 Oct. 1999.

47. The Institute at Biltmore, at http://www.strategicplan.org (accessed 16 Sept. 2003).

48. Gibson, interview.

49. Just, interview, 8 Mar. 2001.

50. "Back the Buyout Campaign Themes," undated list, ESOP Committee archives.

51. Peggy Gosselin, "Mills Dubbed Sunburst Papers," *Waynesville (N.C.) Enterprise Mountaineer,* 27 Mar. 1998, A1.

52. "Back the Buyout Campaign Themes."

53. Ibid.

54. Ibid.

55 Ibid.

56 Sutton, interview, 3 Mar. 2003.

57 Stacey/Rick to Pat Cabe and Dan Ray, "Employee Owned Paper Company Timeline/To Do List," facsimile, 13 Mar. 1998, ESOP Committee archives.

58 Sutton, interview, 2 May 2000.

59 Stacey/Rick to Pat Cabe and Dan Ray.

60 Ibid.

61 Just, interview, 8 Mar. 2001.

62 "Letter of Intent for the Purchase of the Assets of the Canton System," 18 Mar. 1998, ESOP Committee archives.

63 Richard Haney, Alton Higgins, Doug Gibson, interview by the author, 3 Mar. 2003.

64 Gosselin, "Mills Dubbed Sunburst Papers."

CHAPTER 7

1. Rose, "Daily Log," 23 Mar. 1998.

2. Haney, interview.

3. Rose, "Daily Log," 23 Mar. 1998.

4. Ibid.

5. Ibid.

6. Ibid.

7. Ibid., 25 Mar. 1998.

8. Ibid., 30 Mar. 1998.

9. Sutton, interview, 3 Mar. 2003.

10. Peggy Gosselin, "Group Takes Buyout Effort to Capitol," *Waynesville (N.C.) Enterprise Mountaineer,* ESOP Committee archives.

11. Alton Higgins, interview by the author, 19 June 2002.

12. Quoted in Gosselin, "Group Takes Buyout Effort to Capitol."

13. Rose, "Daily Log," 2 Apr. 1998.

14. Higgins, interview, 19 June 2002.

15. Rose, "Daily Log," 2 Apr. 1998.

16. Sutton, interview, 2 May 2000.

17. Rose, "Daily Log," 3 Apr. 1998.

18. Higgins, interview, 19 June 2002.

19. Ibid.

20. Rose, "Daily Log," 3 Apr. 1998.

21. Gibson, interview.

22. "Questions for Mr. Brubaker," notes in ESOP Committee archives.

23. Rose, "Daily Log," 3 Apr. 1998.

24. Higgins, interview, 27 Oct. 1999.

25. Rose, "Daily Log," 3 Apr., 1998.

26. Ibid.

27. Gregg, interview.

28. Gibson, interview.

29. Rose, "Daily Log," 6 Apr. 1998.

30. Ibid.

31. Ibid.

32. Ibid.

33. Higgins, interview, 27 Oct. 1999.

34. Rose, "Daily Log," 5 Apr. 1998.

35. Ibid.

36. Rose, "Daily Log," 7 Apr. 1998.

37. Ibid.

38. Rose, "Daily Log," 8 Apr. 1998.

39. Higgins, interview, 19 June 2002.

40. Rose, "Daily Log," 8 Apr. 1998.

41. Ibid.

42. Haney, interview.

43. Just, interview, 8 Mar. 2001.

44. Rick Nall to Bob Goodale, Dan Ray, and Chris Just, memo, 8 Apr. 1998, "Back the Buyout!" information packet, ESOP Committee archives.

45. "Back the Buyout!" newspaper insert. Stacey/Rick to Pate Cabe and Dan Ray, 13 Mar. 1998, facsimile, "Employee Owned Paper Company Timeline/To Do List," "Summary of Activities to Date," notes, ESOP Committee archives.

46. Meeting notes, undated, ESOP Committee archives.

47. Stacey Stafford to Bob Goddale, 2 Apr. 1998, e-mail, ESOP Committee archives.

48. "Back the Buyout Agenda," 9 Apr. 1998; meeting notes, undated, ESOP Committee archives.

49. Just, interview, 8 Mar. 2001.

50. Adams, interview.

51. Tracy Davis, "Sunburst CEO Likes Mill Employees' Enthusiasm," *Asheville Citizen-Times*, 14 Apr. 1998, B1.

52. Higgins, interview, 19 June 2002.

53. Quoted in Peggy Gosselin, "Champion Stockholders Asked to Back Employee Buyout," *Waynesville (N.C.) Enterprise Mountaineer,* 17 Apr. 1998, A6.

54. Higgins, interview, 19 June 2002.

55. Quoted in Gosselin, "Champion Stockholders Asked to Back Employee Buyout."

56. Ibid.

57. Higgins, interview, 19 June 2002.

58. Tracy Davis, "Sunburst Mill Offer Rejected," *Asheville Citizen-Times,* 17 Apr. 1998, ESOP Committee archives.

CHAPTER 8

1 Gibson, interview.

2 Ibid.

3 ESOP Committee notes, 17 Apr. 1998, ESOP Committee archives; Gibson, interview.

4 ESOP Committee notes, 17 Apr. 1998, ESOP Committee archives.

5 "Sunburst Papers Still Bidding for Champion's Mills," 17 Apr. 1998, press release, ESOP Committee archives.

6 Sutton, interview, 2 May 2000.

7 Haney, interview.

8 ESOP Committee notes, 17 Apr. 1998, ESOP Committee archives.

9 Adams, interview.

10. Frank T. Adams to Alton Higgins and the ESOP Research Committee, facsimile, 8 Apr. 1998, ESOP Committee archives.

11. Higgins, 19 June 2002.

12 Quintin Ellison, "Employees Regroup after Rejection," *Waynesville (N.C.) Enterprise Mountaineer,* 17 Apr. 1998, ESOP Committee archives.

13. Peggy Gosselin, "Buyout Sought Despite Refusal," *Waynesville (N.C.) Enterprise Mountaineer,* 22 Apr. 1998, ESOP Committee archives.

14. Henson, interview; Higgins, interview, 19 June 2002.

15. Higgins, interview, 27 Oct. 1999.

16. Ibid.

17. Rose, "Daily Log," 6 May 1998.

18. Ibid.

19. Higgins, interview, 27 Oct. 1999.

20. Rose, "Daily Log," 6 May 1998.

21. Frank Adams, conversation with the author, 7 June 2000.

22. Rose, "Daily Log," 6 May 1998.

23. Ibid.

24. Ibid.

25. Ibid.

26. Just, interview, 8 Mar. 2001.

27. Rose, "Daily Log," 6 May 1998.

28. Rose, "Daily Log," 29 June, 8, 9, 10 July 1998; Kenny Sutton to John Sweeney, 3 Aug. 1998, ESOP Committee archives; Higgins, interview, 27 Oct. 1999.

29. Higgins, interview, 27 Oct. 1999.

30. Ibid.

31. Gibson, interview.

32. Ibid.

33. Ibid.; "Gov. Hunt Urges Champion CEO to Protect Jobs in Western NC," 24 Apr. 1998, Governor's Press Office, ESOP Committee archives; Higgins, interview, 27 Oct. 1999.

34. Higgins, interview, 27 Oct. 1999; Paul Clark, "Champion Buyout Bid Gets Break," *Asheville Citizen-Times,* 18 June 1998, A1.

35. Gibson, interview; Tim Reid, "N.C. Goes to Bat for Champion Workers," *Asheville Citizen-Times,* 20 June 1998, B1.

36. Alton Higgins to Richard E. Olson, 13 May 1998, ESOP Committee archives.

37. Just, interview, 8 Mar. 2001.

38. Ibid.

CHAPTER 9

1. Rose, "Daily Log," 13 May 1998.

2. Ibid.; Gibson, interview.

3. Alton Higgins to Richard E. Olson, 13 May 1998.

4. Gregg, interview.

5. Higgins, interview, 27 Oct. 1999.

6. Peggy Gosselin, "Champion: Mills Run Until Sold," *Waynesville (N.C.) Enterprise Mountaineer,* 15 June 1998, A1.

7. "Brownfields Letter of Intent," 1st Draft for Review, ESOP Research Committee, Robert Deutsch and John D. Runkle to Bruce Nicholson, 23 July 1998, ESOP Committee archives.

8. Ibid.

9. John D. Runkle to Alton Higgins, Frank Adams, and Bob Deutsche, 3 Aug. 1998, ESOP Committee archives.

10 Ibid.

11 Rose, "Daily Log," 15 Sept. 1998.

12 John Sweeney to Malon Wilkus, 22 July 1998, ESOP Committee archives.

13 Kenny Sutton to John Sweeney, 3 Aug. 1998.

14 "Conference Call/Local 507/KPS/Champion/Goldman Sacs," 5 Aug. 1998, transcript, ESOP Committee archives.

15 Ibid.

16 Ibid.

17 Haney, interview.

18 "Conference Call/Local 507/KPS/Champion/Goldman Sacs."

19 Ibid.

20 Ibid.

21 Adams, interview.

22 Rose, "Daily Log," 15 Sept. 1998.

23 Ibid.

24 Ibid.

25 Ibid.

26 Adams, interview.

27 Rose, "Daily Log," 15 Sept. 1998.

28 Sutton, interview, 2 May 2000; Just, 5 Nov. 2003.

29 Rose, "Daily Log," 15 Sept. 1998.

30 "Term Sheet Agreement between the UPIU and Its Canton System Locals and KPS Special Situations Fund, L.P.," ESOP Committee archives.

31 Ibid.

32 Robert J. Deutsch to Alton Higgins, 4 Oct. 1998, ESOP Committee archives.

33 Ibid.

34 "Term Sheet Agreement."

35 Ibid.

36 Sutton, interview, 2 May 2000.

37 Ibid.

38 Pete Dagostino to members of United Paperworkers International Union, Local 673, ESOP Committee archives.

39 Sutton, interview, 2 May 2000; Pete Dagostino to members of United Paperworkers International Union, Local 673.

40 Sutton, interview, 2 May 2000.

41 ESOP Research Committee to Canton System Employees, 28 Oct. 1998, ESOP Committee archives.

42 Gibson, interview.

43. Higgins, interview, 27 Oct. 1999.

44. Ibid.

45. Ibid.

46. Deutsch to Alton Higgins, Kenny Sutton, ESOP Research Committee, 2 Dec. 1998, ESOP Committee archives.

47. Ibid.

48. Frank Powers and Phil Smith to Mike Psaros, facsimile, 6 Nov. 1998, ESOP Committee archives.

49. Sutton, interview, 2 May 2000.

50. Powers and Smith to Psaros.

51. Ibid.

52. Sutton, interview, 2 May 2000.

53. UPIU Local 507 Employee Stock Ownership Research Committee to Every Canton System Employee and Each of Your Family Members, undated, ESOP Committee archives.

54. Quintin Ellison, "Canton Residents Resigned to Waiting for Mill Sale," *Asheville Citizen-Times,* 11 Jan. 1999, A1.

55. Gibson, interview, 21 Dec.1999.

56. Ibid.

57. Ibid.

58. Haney, interview.

59. Ibid.

60. Ibid.

61. Robert Smith, Alton Higgins, Pete Dagostino et al. to Canton System Employee and Families, 1 Feb. 1999, ESOP Committee archives. See also, "Letter Details Status of ESOP Buyout," *Waynesville (N.C.) Enterprise Mountaineer,* 17 Feb. 1999, A10.

62. Quintin Ellison and Sandy Wall, "Employee Group Tentatively OKs Purchase of Paper Mills," *Asheville Citizen-Times,* 17 Feb. 1999, A1, A4.

63. Quintin Ellison and Sandy Wall, "Environmentalists See 'Win-Win' Outcome," *Asheville Citizen-Times,* 17 Feb. 1999, A1.

64. Sandy Wall and Quinton Ellison, "Champion Buyout a Tough Sell," *Asheville Citizen-Times,* 18 Feb. 1999, A1.

65. "What Do You Think?" *Asheville Citizen-Times,* 18 Feb. 1999, A1.

66. Ibid.

67. Quintin Ellison, "Champion Worker Buyout Vote Nears," *Asheville Citizen-Times,* 7 Mar. 1999, A7.

68. Higgins, interview, 27 Oct. 1999.

69. Alton Higgins, interview by the author, 30 Sept. 2003.

70. Ibid.

71. Ellison, "Champion Worker Buyout Vote Nears," A7.

72. Sandy Wall, "Champion Buyout Plan Would Force Cut in Pay," *Asheville Citizen-Times,* 18 Mar. 1999, A1, A4.

73. "Champion International Corporation Agrees to Sell Canton Mill and DairyPak Operations to the Carolina Paper Company," Yahoo! Finance, 29 Mar. 1999, at http://biz.yahoo.com (accessed 30 Mar. 1999); Sutton, 2 May 2000. Account confirmed by Adams, 8 June 2000.

74. "Champion International Corporation Agrees to Sell."

75. Sutton, interview, 2 May 2000.

76. Frank Adams, conversation with the author, 5 June 2003.

77. Peggy Gosselin, "Champion Buyout Succeeds," *Waynesville (N.C.) Enterprise Mountaineer,* 31 Mar. 1999, A1.

78. Sutton, interview, 2 May 2000.

79. Gosselin, "Champion Buyout Succeeds," A9.

80. Peggy Gosselin, "Local, State Officials Praise Mill Purchase," *Waynesville (N.C.) Enterprise Mountaineer,"* 31 Mar. 1999, A1, A9.

81. Ibid.

82. Gosselin, "Champion Buyout Succeeds," A9.

83. Ibid., A1.

84. "The Southern Appalachian Center for Cooperative Ownership, Inc.," press release, 30 Mar. 1999, ESOP Committee archives; Gosselin, "Champion Buyout Succeeds," A9.

85. Gosselin, "Champion Buyout Succeeds," A9.

86. "CEO Named for Canton System," press release, 1 Apr. 1999, ESOP Committee archives; Peggy Gosselin, "CPC Names New CEO," *Waynesville (N.C.) Enterprise Mountaineer,* 2 Apr. 1999, A10.

87. "CEO Named for Canton System," press release, 1 Apr. 1999, ESOP Committee archives.

88. Peggy Gosselin, "New CEO Meets Mill Workers," *Waynesville (N.C.) Enterprise Mountaineer,* 10 Apr. 1999.

89. Sandy Wall, "Tentative Date Set for Champion Vote," *Asheville Citizen-Times* 2 Apr. 1999, B1; Sutton, interview, 2 May 2000.

90. Sutton, interview, 2 May 2000.

91. Ibid.

92. Peggy Gosselin, "Employees Approve Buyout," *Waynesville (N.C.) Enterprise Mountaineer,* 30 Apr. 1999, A1; Adams, 5 June 2003.

93. Sandy Wall, "Champion Buyout Approved," *Asheville Citizen-Times,* 30 Apr. 1999, A1.

94. Sutton, interview, 2 May 2000.

95. "The Southern Appalachian Center for Cooperative Ownership, Inc."

96. Gosselin, "Employees Approve Buyout," A13.

97. Adams, interview.

98. Haney, interview; Higgins, interview, 27 Oct., 1999; Sutton, interview, 3 Mar. 2003.

EPILOGUE

1. Haney, Higgins, and Gibson, interview, 3 Mar. 2003.

2. Adams, interview.

3. Gar Alperovitz, "Movement Building and the Future of Workplace Democracy." A presentation at the *Eastern Conference for Workplace Democracy 2002*. Aurora Productions C2-11. Audiocassette.

4. Ibid.

5. Ibid.

6. Sutton, interview, 3 Mar. 2003.

7. Ibid., 2 Feb. 2001, 3 Mar. 2003; Daniel Gregg, interview with the author, 22 Apr. 2003.

8. Haney, Higgins, and Gibson, interview, 3 Mar. 2003; Gregg, interview, 22 Apr. 2003.

9. Ibid.

10. Ibid.

11. Higgins, interview, 30 Sept. 2003.

12. Ibid.

13. Ibid.

14. Ibid.

15. Gregg, interview, 22 Apr. 2003.

16. Sutton, interview, 3 Mar. 2003.

17. Gregg, interview, 22 Apr. 200.

18. Haney, Higgins, and Gibson, interview, 3 Mar. 2003.

Index

Under the Workers' Caps was designed and typeset on a Macintosh computer system using QuarkXPress software. The body text is set in 10.5/13.5 ITC New Baskerville, and display type is set in Ocean Sans and Rockwell. This book was designed and typeset by Liz Lester and manufactured by Thomson-Shore, Inc.